WINNIN

job-hunting strategies for first-time job hunters

GARY WOODWARD

APRIL 2006

Winning Job-hunting Strategies for First-time Job Hunters
This first edition published in 2004 by Trotman and Company Ltd
2 The Green, Richmond, Surrey TW9 1PL

Reprinted 2004

Editorial and Publishing Team
Author Gary Woodward
Editorial Mina Patria, Editorial Director; Rachel Lockhart, Commissioning
Editor; Anya Wilson, Editor; Bianca Knights, Assistant Editor
Production Ken Ruskin, Head of Pre-press and Production
Sales and Marketing Deborah Jones, Head of Sales and Marketing
Advertising Tom Lee, Commercial Director
Managing Director Toby Trotman

Design by XAB

British Library Cataloguing in Publication Data
A catalogue record for this book is available from the British Library

ISBN 0 85660 973 0

Typeset by Mac Style Ltd, Scarborough, N. Yorkshire
Printed and bound in Great Britain by Bell & Bain, Glasgow, Scotland

contents

About the author

Gary Woodward is a qualified careers consultant and freelance careers writer. He has written numerous articles for careers magazines and websites, as well as for national newspapers on a wide range of topics. He has significant experience of advising young people on job-hunting strategies as well as helping more experienced professionals with their career development. He is also co-author of the book, *Working in Development: An Introduction*.

Acknowledgements

I would like to acknowledge David Winter for some of the concepts in this book and to thank Neil Roscoe for his support and encouragement.

Introduction

Making job hunting simple

Who needs to read a book on job hunting? Surely it's easy: you look for job ads, you make applications and, hey presto! – you've got a job. Well, you may be fortunate enough to have had that experience in the past, or maybe other people you know seem to get jobs without any problems; but sometimes jobs don't come so easily. However, there are definite techniques you can learn to improve your chances.

For some people, especially those new to job hunting, the whole process can be daunting and stressful. For one thing, there are so many conventions, so many things to think about: what kinds of job to look for, what qualifications and experience are required, how to go about preparing CVs and covering letters, understanding the language of job advertisements, the art of making personal contacts, and so on. However, there are a few things you should try to remember, some of which should make you feel more comfortable straight away.

- You are not alone – there are lots of job-hunters out there
- Employers are always on the lookout for good candidates to fill vacancies
- Job-hunting skills are something that can be learned by anyone and are not the preserve of a lucky few
- Most people don't go about job hunting in a systematic manner. If you do, you will be at an advantage
- On the whole, the job market is in a good position at the moment. At the time of writing (February 2004), the unemployment rate was at 4.9 per cent – the lowest unemployment rate since 1984.

Feel better? Good. This book is about giving you confidence in job hunting and equipping you with an array of skills and techniques to help you land the job you want. It is aimed primarily at those who are new to the job market, or those who may be returning to work after a significant break. Having said that, the techniques described in these pages can be used by anyone, whatever their situation.

How to use this book

To get the most from this book, I recommend reading it through once and then reading each chapter a bit more closely, making notes if you feel that will help. Some of the strategies in this book may be new to you; others you may have heard of before. Whatever the case, you have to implement the techniques and not just think about them. If you are bold enough, and determined enough, to follow through with some of these principles and stick to them, you will get results. One of the reasons you will get results is that you will be in the minority. So see this book as a workbook, an instruction manual, and as you go about your job hunting be sure to record any insights or inspiration in a notebook, journal or palmtop.

The book takes you through the job-hunting process, as well as effective strategies, in a logical, sequential order, reflecting the steps shown below:

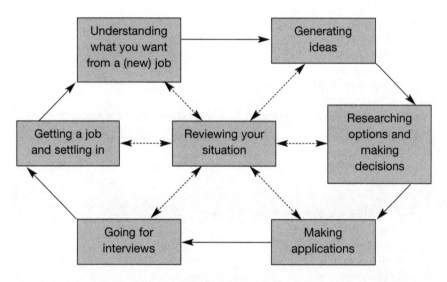

The job-hunting plan

As you can see from the diagram, the process is a cyclical one, and even when you are in a job you will probably review your situation periodically. You don't necessarily have to start at a particular point in the sequence to get a job, but experience shows that those who do some thinking, planning and research before applying for positions are the ones who end up the happiest.

If you are very pushed for time, or you need results very quickly, or you know you need help in just one particular area of job hunting, then by all means focus on that chapter to begin with; but bear in mind that you may have missed some valuable information in other chapters. If you're not sure about your own job-hunting abilities, try the brief job-hunting questionnaire below and then go to the appropriate chapters.

Job-hunting readiness questionnaire

	Job-hunting problem	Which chapter(s)?
1	I need another job, but I don't know what my options are.	2 and 3
2	I know the kinds of job I want to do, but don't know how to find out more about them.	3, 4 and 5
3	I know what I need to do in terms of job hunting, but I can't seem to get organised enough to do it effectively.	1
4	I don't know what my skills are.	2
5	I found some jobs I'm interested in, but need help with filling in application forms.	6
6	I keep getting interviews, but never seem to get the job.	7 and 8
7	I have no idea about what I want to do.	2 and 3
8	I've been through a period of job hunting and nothing has come of it.	8
9	When I have the opportunity to ask people about their jobs, I don't know what to say.	5 and 9
10	I don't know how to use the Internet for job hunting.	4
11	I have no idea where to look for vacancies.	3, 4 and 5
12	I am not very good at 'networking' or developing contacts.	5
13	I don't know anything about job-hunting conventions in the UK.	All the chapters!
14	I have a job offer, but still have some interviews for jobs I really want. What should I do?	9
15	My job hunting seems a bit random and aimless.	1, 2 and 3

1

Job-hunting essentials

This chapter will show you:

- **what you need to think about before you start job hunting**
- **how to come up with a realistic job-hunting plan**
- **how to develop good mental habits.**

It's a cliché that job hunting is a full-time job in itself. Like many clichés, however, there is more than a grain of truth to it. Whether you're looking for your first job or returning to the labour market after a career break, job hunting can demand a lot of your resources. One of the most common errors people make when they embark on this process is that they underestimate what it's going to cost them in terms of time, money and energy. That is why one of the most important steps in the whole process is to come up with a plan and a timetable for your job hunting. You may be tempted to skip this section, but stick with it: it is deliberately brief so that you can grasp the essentials without trying your patience too much!

Your main job-hunting resources

Time

You can't do job hunting in the odd moment here or there. To maximise your chances of success, you need to dedicate a certain amount of time every day, or at least every week, to achieving your goal. Study the following chart before you draw up a schedule for your job search.

Times needed for job hunting

Job-hunting activity	Estimated time needed
Analysing your skills, qualifications, experience and career interests	At least 2–3 days
Generating ideas and researching your career options	One week at least
Making applications	½ day per job
Preparing for interviews	1 day per job
Travelling to and from interviews	Will vary a lot, but allow extra time
Part-time or voluntary work (while you're job hunting)	Try to commit no more than 15 hours per week to this
Social life/other non-job-hunting activities	This will vary from person to person, but try to block out some time to relax and enjoy yourself

Once you've thought about your time commitments realistically and in some detail, try to come up with a target date by which you want to get your preferred job. For some, this may be a long-term project and they are happy to take their time. For others, it's a matter of great urgency and desperation – in which case you will need to commit more of your resources straight away.

Use the following diagram to help you draw up a realistic schedule:

Set yourself a goal or deadline by when, realistically, you need to have a job.

↓

Given the deadline above, work out how much time you need to dedicate per week, or per day, to job hunting. Obviously, the more quickly you need the job, the more time you are going to have to spend on it immediately.

↓

Draw up a job-hunting schedule and allocate the time in your diary or personal organiser for this purpose. Remember, you need to set aside time for things such as analysing your skills, researching, reading job ads, making contacts, visiting employers and so on. Try to be realistic.

↓

Stick to your plan and modify it only if it seems wildly unrealistic once you have started the job-hunting process.

Job-hunting schedule

Money

Much of the job-hunting process can be done for very little money, but you will have to make an allowance for things such as phone calls, Internet bills, stationery, postage, etc. You may also have to consider more long-term investments such as a personal computer (PC), mobile phone or personal organiser.

Do some basic calculations about how much money (if any!) you have at your disposal and then work out your priorities in terms of expenditure. A list of things you need to factor in for drawing up a realistic job-hunting budget might look something like this:

Anticipated expenditure on job hunting	
Job-hunting expenditure	**Amount (£)**
Telephone calls	£5 per week
Internet bills	£5 per week
Postage	£10 per week
Stationery	£10 – purchase when needed
New suit/clothes (optional)	£50 to £200
Personal organiser (optional)	£50 to £300
Personal computer (optional)	£200 to £1000
Transport costs (visiting employers, going to interviews, etc.)	£10 to £20 per week

Clearly, you don't need to go for all the optional extras mentioned here; but by budgeting in this way, you will start to get a clearer picture of what resources you have available to you and what you can afford to spend. This can also affect how long you can continue the job-hunting process, and may also affect the time frame you have allowed.

Space

You need to treat job hunting with respect, and that means setting aside some room for your endeavours. Some kind of office space is ideal; but avoid using your bedroom if you can help it, because it tends to put people in too cosy a frame of mind to conduct job hunting with the businesslike approach it needs. If you do have to use your bedroom, then try and arrange for a corner of it to be dedicated to your job-searching efforts. If you don't have access to any appropriate space, you might want to consider alternatives such as public libraries, Internet cafés, or school or university common rooms. These are not ideal, but sometimes 'needs must'.

Your job-hunting tools

The personal computer (PC)

A large part of job hunting involves writing letters, updating your CV, sending emails and doing Internet searches. Given that you are looking for a job, money may be tight, but if you can afford it a PC may be well worth the investment. It should hopefully pay off not only in terms of making your job hunting more efficient and your applications more professional, but it should also enable you to keep your IT skills honed.

You can pick up PCs second-hand from lots of places, and they will be more than adequate for your needs. If you really can't afford one, then you will have to be more creative:

- Do you know anyone who has a PC that you could use?
- Does your public library have access to terminals and the Internet?
- Does your previous school or university have a careers centre with access to PCs?
- Is there an Internet café nearby that you could use instead?

If you do decide to go ahead and buy one, one additional thing you might want to consider is whether to get a laptop instead of the more usual desktop machine. If you know that you have a dedicated base for your job-hunting activities, then a desktop machine will probably be fine. If, on the other hand, you know that you will have to move from space to space, then a laptop is probably a better investment. Even if you have somewhere regular to work from, a laptop still might be worth considering, because part of any effective job-hunting campaign is about going out and meeting people. Making notes and keeping records as you travel around is often important. Sometimes you will feel like a travelling salesman; the only difference is that you're not selling double-glazing: you're selling you!

The telephone

As well as PC and Internet access, the telephone is one of the key tools in job hunting. Speaking to people on the phone is in many ways more effective than emailing them or sending them a letter. If you haven't got access to a landline, then maybe you might want to consider purchasing a mobile phone. If that's not possible, then think about buying a phone card with which you can make calls from public phones. This is better than trying to find change every time you need to make a call and, so long as you keep the card topped up, will save you the embarrassment of being cut off in mid-conversation because you've run out of small change!

One word of caution: whether you're using a mobile phone or a landline as your main contact number for potential employers, have a professional answerphone message on it. Often – and particularly with mobile phones –

people's answerphone messages are too jokey or casual for job hunting. Something along the lines of the following would suffice:

'Hello, you've come through to Jane's answerphone. I'm sorry I've missed your call, but if you leave your name and number after the tone, I will call you back as soon as I can. Thank you.'

The personal organiser or notebook

It's essential that you keep a record in some way of the people you've contacted, their contact details and the status of the contact (whether it is a good lead, lukewarm or cold). Developing contacts is crucial in job hunting and it would be a very risky strategy to rely solely on your memory. It's not only contacts that you need to make a note of, but any ideas you may have as you go about your business. Often speaking to one person, or reading a piece of information, can trigger a thought about another possible opportunity or place to search. Treat these ideas like nuggets of gold: don't lose them, because sometimes they can lead to great treasure!

It doesn't really matter whether you use a paper-based notebook or an electronic organiser: it's a matter of personal preference. But the one advantage of having an electronic organiser is that you can usually back up your information on a PC to guard against losing it all.

Your mind: developing good mental habits

Job hunting isn't always the most 'fun' thing in the world. There will be times when you'd rather be watching TV or reading your favourite book. It's really important, though, to keep focused and avoid procrastination. A few techniques for developing good habits are given below:

- Do at least one thing towards your job-hunting plan every day. It may be something very minor, such as making one phone call.
- If you really can't face doing any job-seeking activities, tell yourself that you'll just do 15 minutes. Often, once you do that, you'll find that you do more than you had anticipated.

- Keep your files and records in good order.
- Call a friend, tell them what you're going to do and make them promise to nag you until you've done it!
- Avoid concentrating on the 'not urgent and not important' tasks. You may know that the most important thing is to rewrite your CV today, but instead you decide you need to download a new screensaver onto your mobile phone ...!

... and to find out what you want, move on to the next chapter.

Job-huntingtip

It's really important to work out the practicalities in terms of job hunting, but don't fall into the trap of seeing obstacles instead of opportunities. Always have in your mind what you want just a bit more than how you're going to get it. Nine times out of ten you will find a way to make it happen!

2

What job do you want?

This chapter will show you:

- **techniques to help you decide what's important to you in a job**
- **a way of assessing your own skills**
- **techniques for generating careers ideas.**

So you've worked out what you need in terms of resources for effective job hunting; but before you go job-search crazy, you need to know what you're looking for. You may have some clear ideas already about the kinds of job you're interested in applying for; if so, you may want to skip to Chapter 3 to learn how to find out more about them. If you're really not sure what you want from a job, then this chapter will help you.

There are two parts to this process: thinking about the different aspects of a job that might appeal to you, and thinking of careers ideas. Let's go through these two areas separately.

Deciding what you want: values

One of the most crucial elements of choosing a job or a career area is deciding what your career values are. Having a job that is in line with your values is more likely to make you happy and productive. Values are things such as creative freedom, status, high salary, doing a job that has a positive social impact, working with pleasant people, working in a tolerant environment, flexible work patterns and so on. If you are clear in your own mind about what's important to you in terms of values, then when you start job hunting in earnest you will be able to decide more effectively between different options.

Have a look at the following list of values and try to rank them in order of preference from 1 (most important to you) to 14 (least important). This might not be easy, but it's important that you are able to decide between one thing and another. Take your time with this, and go with your 'gut feeling' if you are really struggling.

Which aspects of a job do you value most?

Value	Ranking
Creativity (able to generate new ideas or solve problems)	
Status (being recognised as working in a high-profile job or environment)	
Social impact (doing something that helps individuals or society)	
Autonomy (having the freedom to do things your own way without too much interference)	
Advancement (there is a defined career structure and opportunities for promotion)	
Money (earning, or having the potential to earn plenty of money)	
Security (your job is pretty safe and you don't have to worry about periodically getting a new one)	
Variety (every day involves doing different tasks, meeting different people or working in different environments)	
Power (your job involves being in charge of other people, and you are the one to make the key decisions)	
Interesting subject matter (you are genuinely interested in the job you are doing)	
Colleagues (your workmates are fun to be with and there are opportunities for socialising)	
Supportive (the organisation that you work for is open and tolerant. Your views are sought and respected during decision making)	
Stress-free (you don't have to work under high levels of stress)	
Working hours (you have the option of flexible working; you don't have to work more than the average working week or during unsociable hours)	

Once you've identified the ranking order of these values, look at the top five you have selected and make a note of them in your job-hunting notebook. You may also want to add some of your own that are not on this list. When you start looking at job ads or speaking to people, these values can act as a kind of internal compass and will help you to focus the direction of your job hunting.

Deciding what you want: skills

Everybody talks about skills, but what are they exactly? Skills are the abilities or qualities you develop over time that can be useful for a variety of different jobs. Some of the most common skills you will see being asked for in job ads include:

- good communication skills
- ability to work in a team
- good attention to detail
- being well organised
- showing initiative.

Let's go over these in turn.

Communication skills

Being able to communicate well is important in the vast majority of jobs. Communication skills can mean having a good telephone manner, writing clearly, being able to build a rapport with strangers, making good presentations, being persuasive, being a good listener and so on.

Teamworking skills

Some jobs involve working more or less on your own, but they are pretty rare. In most work environments you will have to work with a group of people to a greater or lesser extent. Teamwork is all about cooperating, supporting or standing in for others if necessary, not being selfish, and communicating with others on a regular basis.

Good attention to detail

Some people do have a natural attention to detail. If you are one of those people who can spot an error in writing a mile off, or who likes checking information to make sure the facts and figures are correct, you probably have good attention to detail.

Organisational skills

Along with communication skills, this is one of the most common requirements mentioned in job advertisements. Being well organised means planning things properly, meeting deadlines consistently, being punctual, being good at dealing with paperwork, and having systems for remembering to do things and for prioritising tasks.

Showing initiative

In an effort to become more and more profitable, in the last decade or so organisations have slimmed down the layers of management. This means that individuals often have to work unsupervised and using their initiative. Sometimes job ads ask for 'self-starters', which means the same as showing initiative, thinking for yourself and getting things done without constantly asking for permission or advice.

These are just some of the most common skills that you will read about and hear about. No doubt, if you think about it, you've probably developed many of these skills already to a greater or lesser extent. Some other common skills can be seen below:

- interpersonal skills (building relationships effectively; getting things done without upsetting people)
- problem solving (being able to analyse situations and propose solutions)
- leadership skills (being able to direct and motivate others and show vision)
- physical skills (manual dexterity, stamina, endurance, strength)
- flexibility (being able to adapt to new situations or respond quickly in a crisis)
- creative thinking (being able to come up with new ideas; lateral thinking)
- research skills (the ability to collect information systematically and present it coherently).

The skills discussed so far are what are traditionally known as 'soft' skills, but you might also need to think about more specific or 'hard' skills, such as the following:

- IT/computer skills (e.g. familiarity with spreadsheets, touch-typing, knowledge of particular software packages)
- knowledge of foreign languages
- scientific skills (e.g. knowledge of laboratory techniques)
- clean driving licence.

Now that you have some familiarity with the language of skills, think back to any experience you've had so far. It might be things you did at school or in higher education; it could be extracurricular activities, sport, social or personal achievements. Many sixth-form students, for instance, do some part-time work in the vacations to earn a bit of money. So, if you've worked in a shop you will have probably had to develop some level of communication skills, you've handled money and you may have worked in a small team. Already you can claim three useful skills. Now, use your job-hunting notebook to make a list of the skills you think you have at the moment.

Once you've done that, look at the table below. Use it as a way of thinking about whether you would like to use a particular skill in a job, or whether you would like to develop it. Again, feel free to add your own.

Name of skill	I have some experience of this	I would like to use this in my future job
'Soft' skills Communication skills Teamwork Attention to detail Being well organised Using initiative Interpersonal skills Leadership skills Physical ability Creative thinking Research skills **Specific or 'hard' skills** IT skills Foreign languages Driving ability Any other specialist knowledge		

Your skills checklist

As with the values exercise, this will help you to make decisions when you come to apply for jobs, and it will also help you to set the direction of your job hunting.

Thinking of careers ideas

By now, you should be nearly ready to get down to some serious job hunting. You know what resources you need and what resources you already have. You have some ideas about what's important to you in a job, and you probably also have a clearer picture of what skills you would like to use in your future job. But you still need to come up with some actual careers ideas and to find out about real jobs.

This next section focuses on how you can think of ideas for jobs and careers.

Using career directories

One of the ways to find some careers ideas quite easily is by using career directories. These are books that usually have an alphabetical listing of different types of job or employer. Some people flick through them at random to get some ideas; others go through them systematically and come up with a short list of ideas that appeal to them. If you use one of these directories, bear in mind your list of values and skills as you consider the jobs. In this way, you will get a sense of whether something is suitable for you or not.

There are plenty of careers directories around, but some of the best known include:

GENERAL
Careers 2005 (Trotman Publishing Ltd)
The A to Z of Careers and Jobs (Kogan Page, 2002)

There are also some online career guides, such as the one hosted at www.trotman.co.uk

FOR GRADUATES
The Hobsons Careers Guide (available from www.trotman.co.uk)
The Target Guide series

Speaking to friends, family and contacts

We will focus on using contacts for job hunting in more detail in a later chapter, but for now it's worth remembering that the people you know are a valuable resource for ideas and information. Without becoming a job-hunting bore, when you speak to these people, always try to find out what they do for a living. On the whole, people love talking about themselves, and at the same time you may be gaining valuable ideas. It's a win–win situation!

Computer/online matching systems

There are a number of computer programs or online systems that ask you a series of questions based on your career interests and then present you with a list of possible jobs, using the information you have provided. This all sounds very simple; but remember that there are many factors that a computer cannot take into account and so these programs and systems should account for just one element of your option-producing techniques. The following are examples of matching systems and online idea-generating programs:

- Prospects Quick Match, at www.prospects.ac.uk. You may need to register. This program is primarily aimed at those who've been through higher education, but it is useful to most people.
- Self-Directed Search® is an online program assessing your interests and personality and relating these to job types. There is a charge for a full report. Visit www.self-directed-search.com
- You can also try the career interest game, hosted by the University of Missouri Careers Center. Visit www.career.missour.edu then click on 'Career Interests Game' (bear in mind that this is American: but many of the job titles will be transferable).
- Try another quiz at www.princetonreview.com/cte/quiz/career_quiz1.asp. Again it is American, but might still be useful.

Having a consultation with a careers adviser

If you've just left school, you may be able to have a chat with a tutor who specialises in careers. If you are at university or have just graduated, you should be able to speak to a professional careers adviser. If you don't have access to either of those, you could see a private careers consultant. A careers adviser or consultant may be able to give you some ideas, and he or she may also be able to offer you an occupational interest inventory – a questionnaire which, when completed, reveals the kinds of job you might be compatible with.

Browsing job ads

Again we will focus on how to read job ads critically in subsequent chapters. The main thing, in order to come up with ideas, is to look at the range of advertisements, irrespective of whether you are qualified for the jobs. Looking at job ads you wouldn't normally consider is also a good way of broadening your horizons.

Surfing the web

There is a wealth of careers information on the Internet. Looking at recruitment websites or careers service websites is a good place to start to add to your bank of job ideas. (See Chapter 4 for further information about this.)

The one-factor method

One way you can generate ideas for yourself is to think about one particular thing that you would like to have in a job. It could be a skill or a value – or maybe even something you *don't* want. For instance, let's say you want a job that involves writing. Some of the things you might come up with are:

- journalist
- novelist
- press and publicity officer
- civil servant
- lawyer
- author of technical manuals
- translator.

This kind of exercise becomes a little bit easier once you have more knowledge of what jobs are out there, so it may be worth revisiting once you've looked through some career directories and gone through the chapter on researching your options.

Job-huntingtip

When researching jobs and looking at advertisements, think about the skills you'd like to use or develop and what your career values are. This will really help you to decide between one sort of job and another.

The pitfalls of 'scattergun' job hunting

Mark, 19, went to see a careers adviser to help him with his job hunting. He had recently completed his A-levels and afterwards had done some travelling overseas. Now back in the UK, he'd been making lots of applications but with little reward, and he was very stressed.

'I've made so many applications you wouldn't believe it,' was his opening statement.

'What sort of things have you been applying for?' he was asked.

'Anything and everything,' he responded.

'That could be part of the problem,' the adviser suggested.

Although Mark seemed puzzled by that response, once things were discussed in more depth it became clear to him and the adviser that he had fallen into the following traps:

■ he had not given any time to planning his job hunting
■ he had not thought about his skills and values when deciding which jobs to apply for
■ he had applied for many things, but without spending sufficient time on his applications.

Some time was spent discussing what was important to him in a job and how to produce some ideas based on the things he enjoyed. It became clear that he was talented with computers and was also good at communicating computer-related concepts to other people. Based on that, the adviser encouraged him to come up with a realistic plan of what he could achieve each week in terms of job hunting. Mark also realised that spending more time on making a handful of high-quality applications might reap more rewards than responding to job advertisements willy-nilly. Shortly after the discussion, he was offered his first job, working in IT training within local government.

Researching careers ideas and finding sources of vacancies

This chapter shows you:

- **how to find out more about careers ideas you already have**
- **the main places where jobs are advertised**
- **how to get the most out of recruitment agencies.**

Let's recap on the stage you should have reached by now. You will have analysed your strengths, skills, values and experience. You should have been able to think of some exciting careers ideas. Now is the time for you to find out about some of the ideas that attract you most, and to discover the most common places where vacancies can be found. Make a list of your top five career ideas and begin with those – otherwise the task might seem extremely daunting!

Before you start researching the different career areas that appeal to you, it's important that you think about what you want to find out. The following list of questions will get you started, but remember to add any of your own that may occur to you:

- What jobs are available in this particular area?
- What do the jobs specifically involve?
- Who are the major employers in this sector?
- What is the salary range for this job?
- What are the working hours like?
- What qualifications, skills and experience are needed?
- Are these jobs limited to certain geographical locations?
- What is the job market like in this particular sector? (E.g. is the number of vacancies growing or shrinking?)
- What is the application process for this particular job?

When you reflected on your skills in a previous chapter, you may have realised that the ability to research was one of your natural skills. If so, all well and good; if not, bear in mind the following when carrying out your research:

- Use a variety of sources
- Build up your contacts
- Think as creatively as possible
- Reflect on your values and skills while you research
- Don't try to research too many areas at once.

Sources of information and vacancies

Careers information and sources of vacancies can be gleaned from both printed and online media, as well as by talking to people. The following is a list of useful sources of careers information.

Careers libraries

There is a wealth of useful information here, from descriptions of the types of job to job-market statistics. As mentioned previously, you may have access to a careers library in your school or university. If not, many local libraries have a careers section. Much careers information is also online, so it may be worth doing a web search for careers libraries to see what turns up. Many careers services and libraries also have job noticeboards or work-experience opportunities.

Job centres

Again, this is often a source of vacancies that many people overlook, thinking that the jobs held here are of a poor quality or somehow sub-standard. In reality, there is a whole range of jobs available and many employers use job centres as a cheaper way of advertising than through recruitment agencies or the local press.

Newspapers: national

National newspaper advertisements do attract a large number of applications. In that sense, you are up against many other people when applying for such jobs. Irrespective of your chances through this method, they are still a really good source of job information, as well as vacancies. Indeed, many national papers produce an industry-related supplement to go with the relevant jobs. This can be a very good source for the latest news, trends and snippets of information in a particular area. The table overleaf gives details of the different job areas covered by the national newspapers on different days.

Job sectors covered by the national press

Job Sector	Monday	Tuesday	Wednesday	Thursday	Friday	Saturday
Administration/ Secretarial	The Guardian Metro	Evening Standard (London)	The Times	Metro	The Times	
Charities/NGOs			The Guardian			
Computing/IT	The Independent		Evening Standard (London)	The Guardian		
E commerce	The Guardian					
Education		The Guardian	The Independent	The Times	Times Higher Ed Times Ed Suppl	
Engineering			Evening Standard	The Guardian		
Environment			The Guardian			
Finance		Metro Evening Standard (London)	The Guardian The Independent			
General				Evening Standard Telegraph The Times		The Guardian
Hotel & Catering		Evening Standard (London)		Metro		

Legal		*The Times*	*The Independent*			
Marketing/PR	*The Guardian*	*The Independent*	*Evening Standard*	*Metro*	*Metro*	*The Times*
Media/New Media/Creative	*The Guardian*	*The Independent* / *Evening Standard (London)*	*Evening Standard*	*Metro*		*The Times*
Public Sector Incl. Health			*The Guardian* / *Metro*			
Sales/Retail	*The Guardian*	*Evening Standard (London)*		*Metro* / *Telegraph*		
Science				*The Guardian*		

Local newspapers

Don't underestimate your local papers, even the free ones. They are a valuable resource, especially if you have decided to live in the local area they cover. Local papers sometimes have certain themes for certain days in terms of jobs, but that is far less common than it is with the nationals.

Professional bodies/associations

The majority of work sectors have different professional bodies or organisations that represent the interests and professional development of people who work in that particular sector. The Association of Plumbing and Heating Contractors (APHC), the Chartered Institute of Personnel and Development (CIPD), the National Union of Journalists (NUJ), the National Association of Screen Make-up Artists and Hairdressers (NASMAH), are all examples of professional associations. Most of them will have a website where you can find out a great deal of information about the profession, and a number of them will have vacancy listings and possible work-experience opportunities, too.

Job-huntingtip

The Directory of British Associations lists most of these professional bodies and organisations.

Trade journals and industry magazines

These publications are aimed specifically at people who currently work (or want to work) in a particular industry. Sometimes these magazines are produced by the relevant professional association, but many of them are independent commercial ventures. Examples of trade journals include:

- *The Health Service Journal*
- *The Grocer*
- *Marketing Week*
- *People Management* (about Human Resources/Personnel)
- *Plastics & Rubber Weekly*
- *Nursing Times*
- *The Caterer & Hotelkeeper.*

The frequency of publication of these magazines varies considerably: some are weekly, others monthly. As with the professional associations, the magazines will provide plenty of industry insights, as well as snippets such as growth areas, which employers are hiring at the moment and so on. Most of the magazines will also have an online version, but you can get hold of the printed magazines from careers libraries or local libraries. Failing that, many of them are sold in shops such as WH Smith, or if they don't stock them they should be able to order them for you.

What's really good about the trade journals is that they usually have a vacancies section at the back. The majority of these jobs are probably aimed at people with some industry experience; however, there are sometimes junior positions you may be able to take advantage of. The good thing about applying for jobs advertised in an industry magazine is that far fewer people read these magazines, and therefore far fewer will apply for the jobs in comparison with those advertised in a national newspaper such as *The Guardian*. So you increase your chances straight away, as well as showing a potential employer that you know a bit about the industry!

Yellow or business pages

Don't overlook the obvious! You can use these directories to find names of organisations that work in a particular sector. Then you could do a web search to find out more about them or about the sector as a whole. You may even want to get in touch with them to find out if they send out any information about themselves, such as marketing materials or an annual report.

Websites

There is a whole section of this book dedicated to job hunting online. At this point, it's worth saying that most people look online only when they are looking for vacancies, but the Internet has masses of information about jobs, too, even on recruitment websites themselves.

Recruitment agencies

This section focuses on recruitment agencies. It's an important section, because they are often neglected or not approached in the right way. They can be very useful for first-time job hunters in terms of gaining crucial skills and experience or 'getting a foot in the door' of a particular industry or organisation.

So what are recruitment agencies? Recruitment agencies – also known as employment agencies and recruitment consultancies – are in the business of placing people in jobs. They match job seekers with job vacancies. Many companies use consultancies simply to pre-select candidates for them, so that they don't have to plough through hundreds of applications themselves. It's often only at the final interview stage that the employer gets involved. Agencies make their money by charging the employer a one-off fee of around 15 or 20 per cent of the new recruit's annual salary. If the appointee leaves the job after only a few months, however, the agency could forfeit the fee. So, if recruitment consultancies are going to be successful, they must put forward high-calibre and, above all, *appropriate* candidates for the positions available. If they don't, they may find themselves going out of business – fast.

General consultancies place people in a wide variety of sectors: secretarial to managerial, actuarial to industrial. However, most agencies tend to specialise in one particular field of work. The staff who work in these consultancies have usually worked in the industry in which they now specialise. Agencies specialise in almost every sector you can think of, including accountancy, the legal profession, sales, the media, teaching, IT, nursing, science, and catering. Specialist recruitment consultancies are also beginning to offer online services. It's now quite common for graduates to submit their CV electronically and for the consultancy to try to match the details with those on their employer database.

How to use recruitment agencies

HOW TO APPROACH THEM AND WHAT TO SAY

It's a good idea to approach a recruitment consultancy as if you were approaching an employer directly. Dress smartly and try to be professional and businesslike. If you create a poor impression with them, do you really think they will want to present you to their client? When you meet the consultant, don't say, 'I've just finished my GCSEs and was wondering if you've got any jobs.' It's much more effective to say something along the lines of, 'I've just finished school and am looking for a position in . . . Here's a copy of my CV, which outlines my relevant skills and experience.'

Consultancies will be hoping to place you as soon as possible and will be looking for evidence of motivation and relevant transferable skills. To increase your chances of success, therefore, you should be clear about three things: the kind of job you want, the particular sector in which you would like to work, and the skills and experience you possess. Long gone are the days when you could stroll into any consultancy and be placed in a good job within minutes.

You will have to sell yourself to a recruitment consultant, as you would to any other employer. Always think in terms of, 'What have I got to offer this sector/employer?', rather than, 'Please find me a job'.

BUILD A RAPPORT

By selling your skills to a consultancy, you will stand a much better chance of establishing a good rapport with the particular consultant who is assigned to your case. Once you have established this relationship, work hard to maintain it. Don't just register and leave them your CV, hoping that this alone will produce magical results. Instead, make a commitment to keep in regular contact with your named consultant to see if any appropriate opportunities have come in. In this way, when the perfect job does appear, there's a good chance that your name will be in the forefront of their mind.

TEMP YOUR WAY TO SUCCESS

Recruitment consultancies handle 'temp' (temporary) as well as permanent vacancies. Many people take advantage of this and temp to earn some much-needed cash while they're thinking about their 'proper career'. Of course, this is a good way to gain marketable skills while you are job hunting, if you can combine the two without suffering burn-out! Remember, too, it is very common for willing and enthusiastic temps to be offered permanent positions. Temping in a field of work in which you are interested could open up many valuable opportunities for you.

Avoiding disappointment

GET ARMED WITH SOME SKILLS

Consultants are not careers advisers. They are not really interested in your long-term career plans. They want to know what you can offer them – NOW. So, to avoid complete disappointment, make sure you can offer them something immediately, even if it's only basic administrative skills. Sometimes recruitment consultancies will offer you free training in new skills, such as how to use certain IT packages (e.g. Powerpoint or Excel). Cash in whenever you can.

USE RECRUITMENT CONSULTANCIES AS ONE PART OF YOUR OVERALL JOB-SEEKING STRATEGY

Effective job seeking usually requires a combination of many different approaches. Don't rely on recruitment consultancies as the sole means of getting yourself a job. Use them in conjunction with making speculative approaches directly to employers, making contacts, searching the web, and all the other ways of finding a job you can identify that have been outlined in the other chapters of this book.

MANAGE YOUR OWN EXPECTATIONS

Some job seekers become disappointed because of their unrealistically high expectations. Recruitment consultancies are unlikely to instantly offer you the job of your dreams. However, they can provide you with a job which will enable you to gain valuable skills and experience which, in turn, could move you closer to your longer-term career objectives. So, whatever kind of work you get, make the most of it.

Watch out for the sharks!

The majority of recruitment consultancies run their businesses ethically and try to do their best for both employee and employer. But beware: some unscrupulous agencies will try to put you in an unsuitable job and rip you off in the process. Here are some tips for avoiding the sharks:

- Beware any agency that tries to charge you a fee for placing you in a job. They are not supposed to charge prospective employees, but some might try and get round this by charging you for CV services or skills training.
- Don't feel pressured into taking a job for which you are clearly unsuitable. A good consultancy will try to make a close match between you, the job and the employer. A bad consultancy will try to fit you up with anything just so that they can get their 20 per cent cut. The pressure to place you in an inappropriate job may be even more intense if the individual consultant is on commission. It may be worth finding this out.
- If the consultant has arranged for you to have an interview with an employer, they should be able to provide you with some relevant information about the job and the organisation. This should make your interview easier. If they don't, you might want to try a different agency.

If you are at all anxious about disreputable agencies, you might want to stick with some of the more established names which have branches throughout the country. It's also worth knowing that most reputable recruitment consultancies abide by the Recruitment and Employment Confederation (REC) Code of Good Practice. Check out the REC web pages – details given below – for further information. The REC site also has an extensive list of recruitment consultancies, and you can search the list in a variety of ways.

Job-huntingtip

Remember to treat recruitment agencies as if they were the employer themselves and keep in touch with them on a daily basis to see what work has come in.

As well as giving guidelines for choosing an agency, the Recruitment and Employment Confederation (REC) website enables you to search for agencies by specialism, location or company name. You will find it at www.rec.uk.com.

Some recruitment consultancies have lost business as a result of online recruitment: that is the subject of the next chapter.

4

Online job hunting

This chapter will show you:

- **_the basics of the Internet_**
- **_how to do an Internet job search_**
- **_the most common recruitment websites_**
- **_how to apply for jobs online._**

In some ways, the Internet has revolutionised job hunting. Job hunters can find information about organisations, vacancies and recruitment agencies at the click of a mouse, rather than having to wade through magazines and newspapers. Recruiters like the web, too, because they can access a larger pool of employees more quickly than ever before. It also reduces their costs, in that they don't necessarily have to produce expensive recruitment literature or pay recruitment agencies to hire people for them.

The slight drawback of the Internet revolution in terms of job hunting is that there seems to be so much information on the web that it can be very easy to become overwhelmed and lose the focus of your job search. So you really need to approach online job hunting in the right way, otherwise you'll spend hours surfing the web without getting a job!

The basics

Most people are familiar with the language of the Internet by now; but for those of you whose minds need refreshing, the following guide is a rundown of web lingo.

- **URL** – short for Uniform Resource Locator – is the address of a page on the Internet (e.g. http://www.trotman.co.uk)
- **http://** – hypertext transfer protocol. This basically tells your browser what kind of document it is and how to translate it
- **www** – the name of the server the site is on
- **trotman** – the name of the particular domain, often the name of the organisation or individual to whom the domain belongs
- **.co.uk** – this indicates that the website is a commercial set-up based in the UK. Other extensions include .com (a commercial enterprise that could be based anywhere, but often in the US), .es (Spanish), .org (an organisation that is not usually profit-making), .net, .biz, .org.uk and so on.

If you know the URL of the website, just type it into your browser, press 'enter' and enjoy a trip in cyberspace!

Using search engines

On most occasions, you won't know the address of a particular site, but simply want to search for a particular job or industry area. This is where search engines are useful. Search engines provide a means by which you can enter a particular phrase or keyword and get results related to that. Internet browsers usually have a search button, and this will either default to a particular search engine or will give you a choice of which search engine you want to use. Some of the most common search engines include:

- Google
- Dogpile
- Lycos
- Altavista
- Excite
- Infoseek.

Some search engines, such as Dogpile, are called 'meta' search engines. This means that they search all of the other most common search engines to find what you asked for.

When you visit a search engine, e.g. www.google.co.uk, you are generally given a box in which to type your search, and you then need to press 'Go', 'Search' or something very similar. Depending on your search words, you will probably get a huge number of results, some of which might be useful, some not. For instance, an entry of the words 'jobs' and 'UK' into the Google search engine currently produces 6,000,000 results! It would be impossible to plough through them all. So try to ensure that your searches are as specific to your needs as you can make them. For instance, if you were looking for a marketing job in Bristol, you could put in the key words 'marketing jobs' and 'Bristol'. This currently produces a result of 69,000 entries – quite a reduction, although still too many to check them all. To be even more specific, search by using a specific phrase. So if you wanted to retrieve results that specifically relate to becoming a plumber, you would enter the following: 'how to become a plumber'. This currently produces just 112 results through Google. If you're concerned about overlooking any options when searching the web, it's probably worth starting with fairly broad search categories to begin with and becoming more and more specific as your needs dictate.

Your search will usually produce a series of links for you to click on. This in turn may take you to other links, which may lead elsewhere. This is the beauty and fascination of the web, but also its curse: hours can pass without your realising it! So before you do online searching, be disciplined about how long you are going to spend doing it and try not to get sidetracked into exploring off at tangents, unless they look really promising.

Finding vacancies on the web

There are many ways to find vacancies on the web – you may find them in the most unexpected places – but the most common places to look are the following:

- job and recruitment sites
- professional bodies
- online versions of newspapers and magazines
- employer websites.

Let's look at each one of these in turn.

Job and recruitment sites

There has been an explosion of these types of site over the last 5 to 10 years. Entrepreneurs have realised that bringing together employers and potential employees is a valuable service where money can be made. There are far too many recruitment sites to list here, but some of the most popular ones at the moment include:

- www.workthing.com
- www.monster.co.uk
- www.alljobsuk.com
- www.fish4jobs.co.uk
- www.totaljobs.com
- www.hotrecruit.co.uk

Many sites ask you to register with them. This is usually free for job hunters, and the motivation on the part of the recruitment site is that they can say to potential employers that they have a large number of people signed up to the site. This in turn makes it easier for them to persuade employers to pay for an advertisement or to post a vacancy with them.

You should also be able to search within particular sites. As with using search engines, try to refine your search if possible. Most sites give you the choice of searching by type of industry, by geographical area, by salary range and so on. When you find a job you're interested in, you can usually apply in several ways:

- by sending your CV and a covering letter, or a completed application form (see Chapter 6)
- by telephone (see Chapter 7)
- by posting your CV onto the website (see later in this chapter)
- by completing an online application form (see later in this chapter).

Professional bodies and online 'trade' journals

As mentioned previously, most sectors of work have a professional body associated with them. The Chartered Institute of Marketing (CIM), for instance, is the professional body associated with that area of work. As well as being a rich source of the latest industry news, many of them post vacancies on behalf of their member organisations. Again, you may have to register and even pay a small subscription for this service, but it could be worth it. Similarly, 'trade' journals – magazines associated with particular professions, such as *Nursing Times* or *The Grocer* – usually have an online version of their magazine which posts jobs. A few examples are:

- www.grocerjobs.co.uk (food)
- www.theappointment.co.uk (retail)
- www.tesjobs.co.uk (education)

Applying for jobs online

Posting your CV

Some recruitment sites simply ask that you register so that they can email you updates of job opportunities etc.; others want to ask for more information about you and your job interests, or maybe even want you to upload your CV. Uploading your CV means submitting it to the website so that it can be viewed by employers. Each site should have clear instructions on how to do that.

This can be a very good service, but make sure the website you are dealing with has good credentials before releasing very personal or sensitive information, and make sure that your details will be kept confidential and not passed on to any third parties (other than the employers). Posting your CV on a site can work, in that employers then find you, rather than you finding the employers. But it can be very tempting to post a few CVs and then expect employers to come chasing after you. This rarely works in isolation – use this option as just one of your many winning job-hunting strategies!

Things to remember when posting your CV on a recruitment website:

- Ensure that your CV is in the correct format before submitting it (you may need to change the layout, length or style of the document).
- If you are submitting your CV for particular jobs or job areas, make sure it is targeted towards those rather than being general. (See Chapter 6 if you need a refresher on CV basics.)
- Ensure that your personal details are not going to be passed on to any third or fourth parties.
- Ensure that you've not posted your CV more than once to the same employer or the same site.
- You may be able to access your 'posted' CV, and therefore it's a good idea to keep it as up to date as possible.

Some employers ask that you submit your CV directly to their website; most of the provisos listed above apply also to this situation. An alternative way of getting an employer to look at your CV (particularly if you are interested in IT-related jobs) is by creating your own website with your CV on it, and then sending the employer a link which takes them directly to it.

Completing online application forms

There is an increasing trend for employers to encourage job applicants to complete online application forms, rather than paper-based ones. Most of the rules that apply for completing a paper application form correctly also apply to online forms:

- Be specific and focused in answering questions.
- Check for spelling and grammar errors.
- Make sure you understand what the job requires before filling it in.
- Complete the form in a way that shows you have the skills or experience to do the job.

(For a fuller exploration of effective CVs and application forms, see Chapter 6.)

However, there are some factors that are unique to online forms that you need to consider.

1 Before you start, try to get a sense of the whole application form. There are often many parts to a form, asking questions about many different areas, and you don't always see this until you have clicked through the whole thing. If possible, print the form out and see what it looks like on paper. If that's not possible, you might want to do a 'dummy run' under a pseudonym, without filling much of it in, to see what the whole thing is like before you start in earnest.

2 Many online application forms allow you to write as much as you like in answer to a question. Keep your answers to the point and full of **relevant** information. Resist the temptation to waffle. Often online application forms do not include a spelling and grammar check. No one wants to employ a person who cannot spell or construct a sentence correctly.

3 Sometimes employers want you to attach a covering letter along with the completed online application form. Resist the temptation of sending only a brief letter because you have completed a form as well. Whenever you send such a covering letter, it's an opportunity for you to 'sell' your skills and abilities and to point out things about yourself that the application form didn't include.

Emailing your CV

As with online application forms, this option is becoming increasingly popular. The advantages are that it's quick and inexpensive for both the employer and the employee. There are certain things you need to remember, however:

- **Never write your CV within the text of an email.** If you do so, more often than not the formatting of your document will become scrambled, and you won't be able to highlight things on your CV the way you can in a Word document. So always attach your CV as a Word document. Call the document something obvious such as your name, e.g. johnsmithCV.doc. (For further information, see Chapter 7 of *Winning CVs for First-time Job Hunters*, Kathleen Houston, 2nd edition, published by Trotman.)
- **Always virus-scan your attachment.** New versions of computer viruses are being produced all the time and, even though the employer should scan it upon receiving it, there is nothing more infuriating than being sent an infected document that could potentially corrupt your computer. These days most machines have virus-scanning software installed on them, but if yours hasn't, either get some quickly or have your document scanned elsewhere.

- **Include a proper covering letter.** People have a tendency to write a very casual covering note within the email that accompanies their attached CV. Make sure your covering letter is as full as it would be if it were on paper. It may even be worth sending both your CV and covering letter as attachments to just a brief email, such as the following:

To: employer@mydreamplacetowork.co.uk
From: johnsmith@hotmail.com

Dear Mr XXXX

Please find attached my CV and covering letter in response to your recent advertisement for the position of administrative assistant.

Yours sincerely

John Smith

Top job-hunting tips when using email

We're all used to emailing, texting and messaging friends in a familiar way, but when you're emailing potential employers the etiquette is completely different. The following guidelines should be useful in this context:

- Treat an email as if you were writing any type of formal correspondence.
- Make sure the subject of your email is clear and unambiguous, e.g. 'application for job as administrative assistant'.
- As with a letter, try to write your email to a named person, e.g. 'Dear Mrs Johnson'. This is important, because sometimes emails are received in one central place and then forwarded to the appropriate person or department.
- Remember to write your name clearly at the bottom of the email so that if it is printed out, your name will stand out.
- Don't necessarily expect a response to an emailed application. It can be frustrating, but it would simply take too long for employers to respond to every applicant saying that they have received their application. If you really need to know something, give it a few days after you sent your email and then perhaps call them by telephone – but don't pester!
- Don't send your CV to a number of employers on the same email. Employers like to think that you are targeting them specifically and not just including them in some random, 'scattergun' approach to job hunting.

- Don't email your CV if it says specifically in the advertisement to apply online or to send your CV and covering letter through the post. It may be more convenient for you to email, but sometimes there's a very good reason why employers want candidates to apply in a particular manner. Completing an (online) application form can take a long time and this shows an employer that you are really motivated to do the job. Taking the easy option does not necessarily impress!

5

Creative job hunting: vacancies in hidden places

This chapter will:

- **introduce the concepts of creative job hunting**
- **show you how to make useful contacts**
- **give you some advice on speculative applications.**

In the previous chapters we looked at the most common sources of vacancies and how to find them. Yet what many people don't realise is that the majority of job opportunities and vacancies are never advertised. Some estimates put the figure as high as 80 per cent! And given that most people aren't actively tapping into that 80 per cent, it means that the vast majority of job hunters are looking for 20 per cent of the jobs. Even for a mathematical novice, those figures don't make good reading! You would be surprised how many employers need people quickly and really prefer not to have to go through a long-drawn-out selection process which can also be quite costly. That is one reason why so many jobs seemed to be filled by 'word of mouth' or by people 'in the know'. This is especially the case in certain areas of work that are very popular, such as the media. If you want to find one of those jobs that never seem to be advertised, then read on!

Creative job hunting is about short-cutting the normal job application process which can be long and drawn out for employers and applicants. Look at the diagram below:

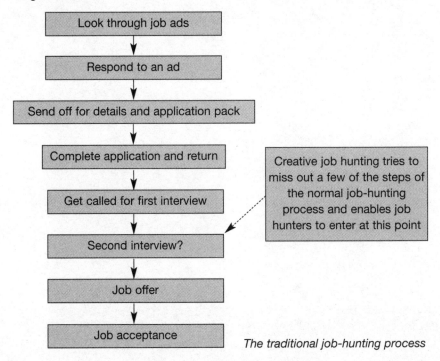

The traditional job-hunting process

You can see that there are quite a few steps to go through; but what creative job hunting does is to miss out some of the steps, to get you an interview or an offer without having to compete against all the other people in the initial stages.

So what does creative job hunting actually involve? It can mean many things, but its usual elements include:

- generating contacts and building relationships (sometimes known as 'networking')
- 'information interviewing'
- reading job ads creatively and critically
- making speculative applications
- 'creative' forms of work experience.

Let's look at each of these.

The art of building contacts

For many people, the idea of generating contacts for the purpose of job seeking is at worst frightening and at best manipulative. But it is a fact of modern life and even once you've got your first job, contacts will prove to be important for a number of reasons. But before we consider how to make new contacts, let's look at the contacts that you already have.

Exercise: Who do I know?

STEP ONE
In your job-hunting notebook, or in the space overleaf, divide the page into four headings:

Family	Friends	Friends of friends	Friends of family

Try and list as many names as you can in each category. To help you a bit, you can flick through your telephone and addresses book if you have one, or look at the contacts stored on your mobile phone. Don't rush this; spend some time until you think you've really dried up. You should be amazed at the number of people you already know, even if there is only a tentative connection.

STEP TWO

The next stage is to think about the job areas you are interested in and see whether any of the people on your list work in that area, or even in a connected area. If they do, put an asterisk or some other identifying mark next to their name. Now, even if no one on your list seems to have any links with any of the areas you are interested in, don't despair. Each and every one of those contacts could themselves know someone working in one of your areas of interest. So from now on, you've got to make it your mission to let everyone know that you're looking for a job, or experience, in a particular field of work. If they're good friends, they may even put the word out to their contacts on your behalf. This is how the whole thing can really build up if you work at it. But remember: networking has to be a two-way process. Try to give something back to people, whether it be the name of a different contact or just a thank-you note. What goes around, comes around!

Developing your network of contacts

Hopefully, once you've done the above exercise properly, you should already have some new contacts and maybe some promising leads. These leads are from people you knew beforehand. What about obtaining contacts from people you don't know at all? That can be quite scary, admittedly, but there are probably lots of situations where you get into conversations with people you don't know. For instance:

- mingling with people at parties or social functions
- chatting to your hairdresser
- meeting new people on holiday
- people you meet through involvement in sporting or other leisure activities
- chatting to people when you're waiting in a long queue for something.

No doubt in the course of conversations with people in these situations it would be fairly simple to ask them what they do for a living and mention the area you're looking to get into. These ideas may appeal most to the more extrovert among you, but having that little bit of courage and making the effort to speak to people – without coming across as a weirdo! – can reap big rewards.

'Information interviewing'

This term was coined by Richard Nelson Bolles in his book *What Colour is My Parachute*, and it basically means asking people about their jobs. The idea is that you approach people in the areas of work you're interested in and ask them if they could spare 10 minutes of their time to talk to you about their line of work. The key at this stage is NOT to say that you want them to give you a job, but more to find out about the area. Clearly this is a very important part of researching and exploring your options, which we discussed earlier, but it's also a good way of making contacts and getting yourself known as someone who's keen to work in that area.

HOW TO DO IT

Information interviewing can be carried out in the following ways:

- Make a shortlist of possible people to contact, whether they be from your personal contacts or from organisations where you might like to work. Try and target the person who actually does the hiring, rather than someone in human resources or personnel. For example, if you wanted to work in the finance department of an organisation, you should try to contact the head of the finance department rather than the personnel office. If you don't know the name of the person, ring up the switchboard and ask them for it.

- Write to the contact or phone them up and enquire whether they could spare 10 minutes of their time to talk to you about their profession/job (remember you're not asking for a job at this stage). You would be surprised at how many people are happy to talk about themselves! During any conversation, if it seems appropriate, it is of course worth mentioning that you're interested in getting a job in this field. If the person you are speaking to doesn't have any vacancies, you could ask them whether they know anyone else who might be hiring at the moment.

- Always have a CV with you, but don't present it to them unless asked to do so; alternatively, leave it with them at the very end of the meeting, after you've established a good relationship.

- Always say at the start how much time you're going to take up and never go over time.

- After the meeting, send the person a thank-you note expressing your gratitude for the time they have given up to speak to you. This one thing in itself has secured jobs for people in the past.

- Write up your meetings immediately afterwards, while the information is fresh in your mind.

- Keep organised records of your contacts, who recommended them to you, when you talked to them and what you discussed.

QUESTIONS TO ASK

Obviously, an information interview is an opportunity not only to make contacts and find out about sources of vacancies; it's also a chance to find out a bit more about the sector you're interested in as a whole. Some questions you could ask include:

- Are there any particular courses or types of work experience which would be helpful?
- What particular skills are the most relevant?
- What are the best ways to go about obtaining the skills, experience, work shadowing, etc., that you need?
- Where do most advertisements for this type of job occur?
- How did you get your job?

It is always a good idea to get your contact to recommend some more people who might be able to offer you further advice. This way you keep your network expanding.

Your contacts database

Some of you may be happy with keeping details of your contacts in a notebook or journal. That's fine. Some of you may want to put the contacts' names and details onto a computer database. The advantage of this is that when you need to find a contact again, particularly if you can only remember part of their name, or where they worked, it's pretty quick and easy to find using the search facilities databases have. The kinds of information you should record about your contacts include:

- name and title of person
- their job function and company
- business address
- telephone and fax number
- email address
- how you got to know this person (e.g. by 'cold calling' or through a mutual friend)
- any useful information this person has given you
- some kind of priority rating in terms of how important you think this contact is to your job search
- any other comments (e.g. reminders of what you or they may have promised to do)
- a space for whether you've sent a thank-you note or not.

Job-huntingtip

Don't reserve your networking efforts only for people who have jobs on offer. Other people may have the contacts that lead you to your dream job!

Reading job advertisements critically and creatively

Most people read only job ads that are directly relevant to them. Sometimes, however, it's possible to get clues about the existence of other possible jobs from reading a wider range of adverts. For example, let's say you were looking for a junior administrative or secretarial position. Why should you bother looking at senior management jobs in the same field? The answer is that when senior managers or directors are hired, the organisation often needs extra administrative support to help them, and these jobs wouldn't be advertised until later, if at all!

In a situation like this, then, you could write to the organisation with a covering letter and CV (see Chapter 6) stating that you noticed that they were recruiting for senior management jobs, and although you're not applying for those positions, you would be interested in any supporting administrative roles. From this point, go on to talk about your relevant work experience and skills, as you would in a normal covering letter.

Work shadowing and volunteering

One of the most underrated ways of making contacts and finding out about vacancies is by getting some unpaid work experience in an area you're interested in. When you write to employers asking for this, don't make it sound as though you are doing them a favour! You still have to 'sell' your qualities to them and set out the reasons why you want to volunteer for them or work on an unpaid basis. You'll be surprised at what you find out when you get on the 'inside' of an organisation. If you're in this position, make sure you make a real effort to build contacts and keep a note of their names.

Making speculative applications

Speculative applications are really just applications you make to an organisation for something that hasn't been advertised. You could be looking for a job opening, a chat with someone about their job, or for some unpaid work experience. Whereas in a standard covering letter, you might start by writing: 'I would like to apply for the position of ...', in a speculative letter you might start by saying, 'I am writing on a speculative basis to enquire whether you may have any openings in the area of ...'. From that point on, you continue as if writing a regular covering letter.

Other key points to remember about speculative applications are:

- Try to address the letter to the person responsible for the department you're interested in, not to Human Resources.
- Always be very clear about what you want.
- Offer examples of your skills, personality and work ethic.
- Show some knowledge of and interest in the organisation.
- If you don't hear anything, follow up your speculative letter with a phone call a few days after you've sent it.

FOLLOWING UP SPECULATIVE LETTERS
The majority of people don't follow up speculative letters – that is why you must do so! Making a phone call a few days after your letter is always a good idea. Even if you don't get a positive response, it gets you used to talking professionally on the phone and shows any potential employer that you have initiative.

An example of the type of thing you could say is:

'Hello, could I speak to … , please?' [Once you've been put through to the right person:] 'Hello, my name is XXX, and I wrote to you a few days ago about the possibility of getting some work experience with you. I'm sure you're very busy, but I was just wondering whether you'd had a chance to give my request any consideration yet.'

Then take the conversation from there. If you can't get to speak to the right person straight away, or at all, try calling early in the morning or late in the evening. The logic behind this is that most managers have a personal assistant (PA) of some kind who will probably screen their calls for them during office hours. Most managers will also usually be in before and leave after their PAs, so that's the time when their calls should be put straight through to them.

Be as creative and daring as you like!

Michael

Michael, 18, desperately wanted to work as a reporter for a newspaper. The difficulty was that he didn't have any work experience. Initially, he replied to ads offering traineeships as journalists, but even those required some experience and he figured he was competing against lots of people who had already done some work in the area.

'I made over 50 applications and got nowhere. Then I got a bit down in the dumps; but not long after that I decided to try a different strategy. I had always been a bit reluctant to use any personal contacts before, thinking it was somehow cheating, but my uncle used to be a journalist and I'd always thought of asking him if he could help, although I never had done so before. So I plucked up the courage to ring him up and asked him whether he still had some contacts on the paper he used to work on. He gave me a few people to speak to and I rang them up, trying to persuade them to let me get a couple of weeks' experience with them. One of the contacts agreed and I did all sorts of work there, from photocopying and making tea to taking notes and answering the telephones. While I was there I also took the initiative to interview a number of people on the streets to get their views about the newspaper and put together a little report for the editor, which he found useful. Although there weren't any openings for junior reporters at the time, he encouraged to me apply later on in the year when there would be an opportunity.'

Later on, Michael did apply and was offered a position. This is a good example of the power of using contacts and taking the initiative.

6

Making winning
applications

There comes a point in job hunting when you've done a lot of self-analysis, you've generated lots of ideas and you've found some really exciting vacancies to apply for. To make your job hunting successful, you therefore need a good CV and you need to know how to complete application forms effectively. As well as looking at answering application-form questions, and showing you how to read job ads carefully, this section will also run through the basics of CVs and covering letters. For a full exploration of CVs, it might be worth investing in a copy of another book in this series, *Winning CVs* (2nd edition), by Kathleen Houston, published by Trotman.

CVs: the basics

Think relevant experience, think skills, think clear layout. In a nutshell, that's what you have to do if you want to put together a good CV. That said, there isn't one 'right' way of compiling a CV (and be suspicious of anyone who tells you there is). Yet there are conventions and top tips definitely worth knowing about.

WHAT HEADINGS SHOULD GO IN MY CV?
Again, there are no hard-and-fast rules, but in general it's usual for a CV to have the following sections (not necessarily in this order):

- personal details
- education
- work experience
- specific skills (e.g. languages or IT)
- interests and activities
- referees.

HOW LONG SHOULD MY CV BE?
This can vary, but most employers will probably start to get bored if your CV is longer than two sides. If you find that your CV is three or four pages long, you may have fallen into the trap of listing lots of information vertically, or waffling or not using space efficiently.

Maximising the impact of your CV

GIVE RELEVANT INFORMATION THE HIGHEST PRIORITY

Who says that education must always come before work experience? If you wanted a job in retailing, for example, and you've already worked part-time in a shop, employers might be just as interested in that as in what you've studied. Always ask yourself what is the most relevant thing you have to offer, and then give it the highest priority on your CV. Busy employers will not always make it to the second page of your CV if there's nothing relevant on the first. If any information on your CV is not at all relevant, you should consider leaving it out.

DESCRIBE YOUR EXPERIENCE IN SUFFICIENT DETAIL

Whether you are explaining education, work experience or hobbies and interests, give enough detail, so the employer can get an idea of the scope of your activities. If you've worked for Sainsbury's, don't dismiss this potentially valuable experience by mentioning it as 'a part-time job while studying'. Describe your work activities, including achievements and responsibilities. If you worked in a team, how big was the team? If you were responsible for a budget, how much money was involved? As with application forms, being too general when describing experience is one of the biggest CV sins.

DRAW ATTENTION TO TRANSFERABLE SKILLS IF NECESSARY

Many people find themselves in the position of having valuable experience, but it's not directly relevant. That's where transferable skills can come in handy. Transferable skills are the abilities or aptitudes you've developed in one context but which can be applied to another. Let's say you've got some experience as a waiter. You could argue that you've developed good customer service skills, the ability to work in a team, insight into how a business works, the ability to work under pressure and so on. All of these are valuable skills to have in the retail management environment, for instance. One note of caution about using skills, though: always use evidence to back up your claims. Try and resist the temptation to simply list lots of skills without saying how you developed them.

WORK ON THE 'COSMETICS' OF THE CV

Have clear, distinct sections for the information. Check and recheck for spelling and grammar errors (don't rely on a computer spellchecker!). Present the information in a consistent manner. Remember: some employers are very fussy about layout and presentation. Avoid the most common spelling errors, for example:

- driving license (should be driving licence)
- liasing (should be liaising).

Use good-quality white or off-white paper. Put each page of your CV on a different sheet of paper, not back to back.

SEND IT TO THE RIGHT PERSON
Irrespective of how your CV looks, its power can be greatly enhanced by sending it to the right person. This is particularly the case if you're sending out your CV speculatively (not in response to an advertisement). Don't just send it to the HR department. Find out the name of the manager in charge of the department you're interested in and send it to him or her. If you know someone already working in the organisation you're interested in, ask them if they would be prepared to present your CV to the relevant person. Using strategies like this will really improve your success rate.

Things to avoid

READY-MADE CVs
Many word-processing packages contain templates of CVs. They can be helpful to get you started, but a CV is your document and you need to say what *you* want to in whatever order *you* think best: not what the template dictates. Employers can recognise this sort of 'manufactured' document a mile off.

SENDING CVs WITHIN AN EMAIL
You will probably have an opportunity to email your CV to an employer. The best way of doing this is to attach it as a document – the layout will be destroyed if you send it as text within your email. However, remember to virus-scan your document before sending it. Just in case the employer has trouble opening your attachment, it's also worth sending a hard copy to them. For more information on online applications and emailing CVs, see Chapter 5.

CV grey areas

PERSONAL PROFILES

Over the last few years there has been a trend to put a 'personal profile' or a section called 'career objectives' at the top of a CV. The purpose of this is to give employers a snapshot of your personality, career and life to date and aspirations. Whilst some employers like them, others find them bland and irritating, particularly if they make generalised claims. Personal profiles are most appropriate for people with quite a lot of work experience and/or people wanting to change careers. If you want to mention your career objectives but don't like the idea of a personal profile, it's the kind of thing you can legitimately put in a covering letter.

PHOTOS

Some people like to attach a passport-size photo to their CV to make it stand out from the crowd. It's a gamble, irrespective of how nice the photo is! Some employers don't like photos on a CV, while others may be more impressed. If you do choose to include a photo make sure it's of good quality, because your CV will be photocopied.

Winning covering letters

Covering letters are a very important part of the application process. Many people are never quite sure what to write in them. Basically a good covering letter includes the following:

- who you are and what you're applying for
- what skills, experience and education you have that are relevant to the job you're applying for
- why you are applying for this particular sector of work
- why you are applying to this particular organisation.

The following template will give you a good idea of how to go about this in detail:

Your covering letter should not exceed 1 side of A4 in length. You should not use a font smaller than 10 or 11 point.

First line of your address
Second line of your address
City/County and postcode

Today's date

Title (e.g. Mr, Mrs, Miss, Ms, Dr), initial and surname of person you are writing to
Their position (e.g. Recruitment Manager)
First line of their address
Second line of their address
City/County and postcode

Dear (Mr/Mrs/Miss/Ms/Dr/Prof) Surname, **or** Dear Sir/Madam (if you have been unable to find name of person to address letter to)

Subject (e.g. Trainee marketing administrator). Quote vacancy reference number if given (Ref. ABC)

First paragraph – Introduction:
- Why you are writing (e.g. 'I am writing in response to your advertisement in the 30 September edition of the Daily News for the position of trainee administrator').
- Who you are ('I will be completing my A-levels in June, and am now very keen to establish a career in marketing').
- Refer to CV if enclosed (e.g. 'Accordingly please find enclosed my Curriculum Vitae for your consideration').

Second paragraph – Why you want the job:
This paragraph must be tailored to the specific job and company you are applying for. There is no such thing as one good, standard covering letter to be sent to all companies! Employers are used to clichés which say nothing specific about them (e.g. 'because you are a leading figure', 'at the cutting edge of the industry') – they immediately recognise that you're probably using exactly the same phrase for 19 other companies!

- What attracts you to this particular company? (Show your research into them.)
- What attracts you to this particular job in this company? (Look carefully at the job description and pick out what makes this job especially appealing.)

- *Why do you want to work in this sector? (You might refer to relevant experience or study. Talk about what makes the sector interesting to you – e.g. does it make use of particular strengths you have? Is it particularly varied?)*

Third paragraph – Why they should be interested in you:
- *Avoid unsubstantiated lists of skills in this paragraph – just stating that you have a skill won't convince anyone that you really do have it. Give evidence!*
- *Your covering letter highlights your main selling points relevant to this employer, so it will be drawing on material contained in your CV – but avoid using exactly the same phrases used in your CV.*
- *Pick out the three or four most important qualities the employer is asking for. What evidence can you give for these?*
- *Mention relevant experience or study (if not already referred to in previous paragraph).*

NB: The second and third paragraphs can be swapped around, according to which order you feel is better for the particular letter you're writing.

Fourth paragraph, if applicable – Extenuating circumstances:
Deal with any negative points of your application which can be justified (for instance poor academic results because of ill health or family problems). You do not need to go into more detail than you feel comfortable giving, but if you don't at least tell an employer that there are solid extenuating circumstances, they will not be able to take them into account and will only take what's on your application at face value. You might also be able to portray such difficult times in a positive light by referring to the personal qualities you needed to overcome them (for instance stamina and perseverance).

Final paragraph – Conclusion:
- Cover any practical issues to do with availability for work or contact details (e.g. dates you will be available for work experience, or dates when you will be at term, and vacation addresses).
- Perhaps refer to your availability for interview (e.g. 'I would be available for interview at any time, except for the week commencing 1 May').
- Sound positive – you might want to thank them for considering your application, or say you look forward to hearing from them.

Signing off:
Yours sincerely *(if addressing named individual at top)* or Yours faithfully *(for Dear Sir/Madam)*

Your signature

Your name

It's worth remembering that while many applicants can show similar experience (or lack of it!) on their CV, a good, interesting covering letter can make your application stand out from the crowd.

Winning application forms

Many of the principles behind effective CV writing apply also to filling in application forms correctly. There are three main areas on an application form:

BIODATA

This is the biographical information you are asked to provide, including things such as your date of birth, education, experience, skills and training, and so on. This part is relatively straightforward so long as it's done clearly and truthfully. Check and recheck for spelling and grammar errors.

SPECIFIC QUESTIONS

Some application forms contain specific questions about skills, sometimes called 'competencies'. An example would be: 'Describe a time when you worked well as part of a team,' or 'Describe a time when you had to deal with a difficult situation.' The key thing with these kinds of question is to be as specific as possible and answer each part of the question if application. A common mistake when answering questions about teamwork, for instance, is being much too general. Look at the examples below:

Bad example:

> Working well in a team means communicating well and supporting each other at all times. It's also important to know what everyone else in the team is doing.

You can see from this example that the person has merely described teamwork, and has not provided a specific example of when they have worked in a team.

Better example:

> When I was at school, I was a member of the school football team. On one occasion, we had a very important match against a nearby school. To make sure we were well prepared, we each said what our particular role was on the field and I made a special effort to encourage other team members during the game. We won 3–0!

This is better because the person has been much more specific about a time when they took part in a team. It also gives the opportunity for an employer to ask about it a bit more at an interview.

'ANY OTHER INFORMATION' SECTION

This can be quite an intimidating section. After you have filled in your biodata and maybe answered some tricky questions, there is often a big blank space for you to 'add anything in support of your application'. If you're not sure what to write here, it's a good idea to think about the kinds of skills or qualities wanted in the job and see which of them you've already addressed elsewhere in the application form. Identify anything you haven't been able to demonstrate so far and try and outline it in this section. Failing that, talk about your motivation and interest in doing the job. Sometimes breaking this section into sub-headings can also help you to structure it better in your mind and on paper.

Fleet Coordinator/Administrator

South London Newspapers, part of the Newsquest Media Group and publisher of the South London Guardian and Comet Series, is looking for a Fleet Coordinator/Administrator to join its busy finance department.

You need to:

■ *be enthusiastic, proactive and willing to learn and take on new responsibilities*
■ *have excellent communication and organisational skills*
■ *have good Excel, Word and email skills and preferably have knowledge of Microsoft Access*
■ *Have GCSEs grade C or above in Maths and English, or the equivalent.*

This position would be ideally suited to an individual who has had previous fleet-management experience, although this is not a prerequisite. The candidate must be reliable, flexible and a team player who can communicate confidently at all levels within the business. In addition, there will be a requirement to undertake some administrative duties within the finance department.

> *Applicants should write, enclosing a full CV and current salary details, to:*
>
> *The Financial Controller*
> *South London Newspapers*
> *34–44 London Road*
> *Morden*
> *Surrey SM4 5BX*
>
> *The closing date for receipt of applications is 30 June.*

This particular job happens to require application by CV, but whether it is by CV or by application form, the key thing is to reflect in the CV, covering letter or application form those qualities listed in the advertisement. When you do this, don't focus only on the ones that have been emphasised by bullet points; try to read between the lines of the rest of the advertisement and imagine what other skills are needed. It says, for example, that the successful applicant will also have to 'undertake some administrative duties' as well as the main job. Bringing out any administrative skills on your CV or application form would be appropriate, therefore.

You shouldn't rule yourself out of job opportunities if, like this one, the ad says something along the lines of 'ideally the candidate will have experience in this area'. Job ads are really statements of 'in an ideal world, this is what the candidate would be like'. Rarely, though, does anyone have all the qualities needed. So put yourself forward, even if you don't meet every single criterion; but avoid applying for jobs for which you don't meet any of the criteria – it's a waste of everyone's time.

CV, application form and covering letter checklist

Use the following checklist as a way of monitoring the quality of your applications:

Checklist for job applications

Question	Yes or No
Have you used your CV/application form/covering letter to show that you have the skills to do the job?	
Have you checked and double checked for spelling and grammatical errors?	
Have you given the most relevant experience the highest priority on your CV?	
When completing your application form, have you answered all parts of the questions in a specific and focused way?	
Does your covering letter mention something specific about why you want to work for that particular organisation?	
Is your CV no more than two sides long?	
When you hold your CV and covering letter out at arm's length is there a nice balance between 'white space' and text?	
Have you told the truth on all your applications?	

These are not all the questions one could pose about applications, but if you've answered 'Yes' to all these, you should be in pretty good shape. If you've got a few 'Nos', reread the chapter!

7

Winning interview technique and other selection methods

This chapter will:

- **show you how to prepare properly for an interview**
- **give you tips on how to answer interview questions effectively**
- **show what may be involved in other selection methods used by employers.**

Part 1: Interviews

Another book in this *Winning* series covers interview techniques so, as with CVs, this section will focus on the basics of getting through an interview successfully, as well as looking at other selection methods.

Successful interview technique basically comes down to remembering the three Ps:

- preparation
- performance
- post-interview analysis.

Preparation

There are three main areas you need to think about when preparing for an interview: yourself, the job and the organisation. Let's look at these in turn.

KNOWING YOURSELF
You should have done a lot of this already in the earlier chapters of this book, but the key areas to think about in this regard are recognising your strengths, weaknesses, skills and experience. It's also important to be familiar with the information contained on your CV, application form and whatever other documentation you used to apply for the job. Make sure you photocopy your application before submitting it.

KNOWING THE JOB
Understanding as best you can the specific job you're applying for is really important. Read and reread the advertisement, person specification and job description thoroughly. Look on the organisation's website to find out more and find out information about similar jobs on other websites. It's even

possible to have an informal chat with the employer about the precise nature of the job before you apply. Not only does this give you useful information, it shows the employer that you have initiative.

KNOWING THE ORGANISATION

As well as knowing about the job you're going for, do some research about the wider nature of the organisation. Who are its competitors? Which direction is it going in? Has it been recently in the news? How many people does it employ? What products or services does it provide? You should be able to find out much of this information from things such as company websites, annual reports, trade journals and newspapers.

Performance

What does 'performance' during an interview mean? Basically, you can break it down into three main elements:

PHYSICAL APPEARANCE AND BODY LANGUAGE

Studies vary on the importance placed on body language during interview situations. However, they all agree that it's a very large part of how an interviewer makes a judgement about a candidate (subconscious or otherwise). Some suggest that interviewers base between 50 and 70 per cent of their judgements on physical presentation and body language. So what is effective body language? It is really about making a good first impression and thereafter avoiding extreme gestures. When you walk into an interview room, make sure that you make eye contact with and smile at all the interviewers, and shake their hands if they are offered to you. From that point on, try to strike a balanced approach in everything you do: a balance between speaking and listening; between making regular eye contact without staring; between giving a firm handshake without squeezing or being too limp; between not leaning too far forward and not slumping back in your chair. Even the clothes you wear should avoid extremes, unless you are going for a job in an industry that puts a premium on flamboyancy and flair! Try to get a sense of what people wear in the organisation you're applying to (often shown in corporate brochures) and adopt something similar.

CONTENT AND STYLE OF YOUR ANSWERS

The content of your answers should be taken care of if you have prepared properly, but what you say can be greatly enhanced or, conversely, weakened by how you say it. Vary the tone of your voice, sound enthusiastic and try not to make your answers too long-winded. If you're not sure if the interviewer wants to hear more on a particular subject, ask them if they would like you to continue.

YOUR QUESTIONS

What questions should you ask them? Try and avoid things that are very obvious and things that you should already know from your research. On the other hand, if it's not clear what the job actually entails, then you should try to find out a bit more. Leave questions about holidays, 'perks' and salary until after you've been offered the position – you are in a much stronger negotiating position at that point. Questions that you might want to ask include:

- How will my performance be assessed?
- Could you tell me a little bit more about the team I might be working with?
- What do you like about working here?
- Is there any scope to take on additional responsibilities in this role?

If at the end of the interview you haven't been told when you are likely to hear the outcome, you are well within your rights to ask. Something along the lines of 'Do you have any idea when I might hear the outcome of the interview?' or 'What's the timing for letting people know?' should do the trick.

Post-interview analysis

If you don't get the job, it's worth trying to get some feedback from the employer. You may not always get it, and if you do, don't expect it in writing – it's simply too time-consuming. Ring up and say that you really want to improve your interview performance and wondered if they could give you some constructive feedback. If you can't get any feedback, try to analyse objectively how things went and where you could improve in the future. Not many people take this step, so doing it usually brings rich rewards in the long run.

Types of interview

There are many different styles and types of interview that you may experience during the job-hunting phases of your life. They may vary by sector, according to the level of the job, or even depending on which people happen to be interviewing you at the time. The main ones are as follows:

(INFORMAL) ONE-TO-ONE

Interviews for many jobs consist simply of an informal chat. While it's certainly nice to be put at ease and made comfortable, don't fall

Interviewtoptip

However informal an interview seems, always act in a professional and courteous way, providing examples of how you can do the job you're being interviewed for.

into the trap of not taking it seriously. During this kind of interview, you might get asked about your previous experience, skills, and interests.

PANEL

This style of interview may seem very intimidating. You face a panel of interviewers (usually all seated behind a desk) and each of them may ask you questions in turn.

Alternatively, one person may ask the questions and another may be making notes on your answers.

Interviewtoptip

During a panel interview, give the majority of eye contact to the person asking the questions, but occasionally look at the other members of the panel too. Divide your attention about 80/20 in favour of the person asking the questions.

TELEPHONE

Many employers use telephone interviews, because it's quick and inexpensive. It's also a good way of weeding out a lot of people early on. This method is used particularly if using the telephone is part of the job you're applying for (e.g. telesales, receptionist work or working in a call centre).

Interviewtoptip

You usually get warning of a telephone interview, so prepare for it as you would normally. Remember that the person on the other end of the phone will be missing your non-verbal clues and expressions, so make an effort to speak a bit more clearly and more slowly than normal.

GROUP INTERVIEWS

Sometimes employers may want to conduct some form of group discussion or exercise as a way of interviewing all the candidates at once.

Interviewtoptip

Don't dominate the group; try to see the other members as allies rather than competitors.

Types of question

As well as different types of interview, there are also many different styles of question. The main ones are as follows:

BIOGRAPHICAL

These are basic questions about you and the facts about your experience, such as what qualifications have you got and so on.

Interviewtoptip

Even if you're asked a supposedly 'biographical' question, such as 'Tell me about yourself,' don't launch into a monologue about your life history. Instead, pick one or two experiences and use them to illustrate that you have the skills or potential to do the job you're applying for.

COMPETENCY QUESTIONS

This is an increasingly common form of questioning. The purpose of these questions is to look for evidence of a particular skill or potential that you may have gained from any experience you've had in your life so far. Typical questions include: 'Can you give me an example of when you've worked well in a team?' or 'Describe a time when you've used your initiative.'

Interviewtoptip

Try to think in advance about the kinds of skills the interviewer might be looking for, and then try and keep in your mind at least two examples for each skill. In this way you won't be flummoxed if the interviewer asks for more than one example of the same skill.

SCENARIO-BASED

Sometimes called hypothetical questions, these make the candidate think on their feet and say what they would do given a certain situation or scenario. For instance, if you were applying for a customer service job, you might be asked: 'Imagine that you are at work and all of a sudden you are confronted by a very angry customer. What would you do?'

Interviewtoptip

Take your time and trust your own judgement. The 'common-sense' answer is usually the best one.

FUNNEL QUESTIONS

This style of questioning gets more and more specific with each question. So you may be asked a general question such as 'What do you like doing in your spare time?' You may answer 'I like reading.' The interviewer may then ask follow up questions such as:

Interviewtoptip

Be truthful about information you put in your CVs, application forms and covering letters!

- What kind of books?
- What was the last book you read?
- Who is your favourite author?
- Who is your favourite character created by that author?

As much as testing your integrity (i.e. have you been truthful about your hobbies and interests?), it's a way of seeing how you react under a bit of pressure.

Other questions you may get asked at an interview

- Why do you want this job?
- What other things are you applying for?
- What do you know about the organisation?
- What are your strengths and weaknesses?
- Where do you see yourself in five years' time?

No matter what question you get asked at an interview, no matter how bizarre, just remember that interviewers are only trying to get evidence to satisfy three important questions:

1 Can you do the job? (i.e. have you the skills, experience, potential, etc.?)

2 Will you do the job? (i.e. are you genuinely motivated, as well as able?)

3 Will you fit in? (i.e. are you easy to get along with and won't annoy other team members?)

Part 2: Other selection methods

An employer's selection process will normally consist of, as a minimum, a written application (either a CV and covering letter or an application form) and an interview. However some employers, particularly for competitive graduate schemes and internships, introduce further selection methods, which you may not be so familiar with. For school leavers, these tests are not particularly common, but they may happen in some areas and are sometimes used by recruitment consultants on behalf of their clients.

Psychometric tests

There are two main types:

- aptitude tests, which assess your abilities
- personality questionnaires, which give a profile of the kind of person you are.

Psychometric tests can be used at various points in the selection process. Sometimes they are used as the second stage of selection – increasingly now as an online test – after the candidate has successfully completed the first written stage of their application, and as a basis to determine which candidates are invited to interview. Sometimes they are used further on in the selection process, possibly after a first interview stage.

APTITUDE TESTS

The most common forms of test are verbal, numerical and spatial/ diagrammatic reasoning. Tests usually take the form of multiple-choice questions, given under exam conditions with strict time limits. There will be definite right and wrong answers. The tests are designed to assess your ability, rather than your knowledge. So the numerical tests assess your ability to understand and use numbers, rather than whether you know how to do algebra or quadratic equations; while the verbal tests assess your comprehension of a given passage, rather than your outside knowledge. The spatial/diagrammatic tests assess your logic and ability to recognise and predict patterns.

PERSONALITY QUESTIONNAIRES

These look at how you tend to react in different situations and they also explore your personal qualities. In contrast to the aptitude tests, there are no set right or wrong answers and usually the questionnaires are not timed. Although the employer will probably be looking for you to show certain qualities that are important to the job (for instance, persuasiveness would be valuable in a sales job), they will not have a rigid profile they are looking for. The best approach is therefore just to be yourself. If you try to second-guess what the employer is looking for, your answers may well come across as inconsistent, which would suggest you are not being wholly honest. Don't worry about these tests too much – putting down your first reaction to questions is usually best, rather than fretting about them.

MORE HELP

As well as getting help from your school or university careers service on psychometric tests, you may also find the following websites useful (both in explaining the tests and in giving you practice examples to try):

www.shldirect.com
www.ase-solutions.co.uk/support.asp?id=62
www.psychtesting.org.uk

Written exercises

Although written exercises take a variety of forms, there are some general principles which apply and some useful steps you could take to prepare:

- Normally, written exercises will be conducted under timed, test conditions – so pace yourself
- Make sure you read and follow all instructions carefully
- Be careful with your grammar and spelling
- Ensure you know how to set out a business letter correctly
- Comprehension is an important part of many written exercises, so practise reading newspaper and magazine articles quickly and summarising their main points.

IN-TRAY EXERCISES

Designed to reflect the kind of work you might typically have to deal with in the job, in-tray exercises test your ability to prioritise and deal with a busy workload effectively. You will be presented with the contents of a fictional in-tray – this will include communications in a variety of forms (e.g. emails, phone messages, letters and internal memos). You will have to decide in what order to tackle the contents of your in-tray in a scenario where you only have a limited amount of time available. You will need to give the reasons for your decisions. You will also probably have to outline how you intend to respond to each piece of correspondence, or at least the most urgent ones.

DRAFTING EXERCISE

You will be presented with a scenario that you have to draft a response to – this will often be in the form of a letter, but could also be an email, press release, article or report. As well as testing your written style, accuracy and structure, such an exercise also assesses your ability to present an argument tactfully and persuasively, tailoring your approach appropriately to your audience.

PROOFREADING

You are most likely to get this kind of exercise for a job where you will have to read others' writing critically (for instance for a position as an editorial assistant in publishing). You will need to correct errors in a passage – so attention to detail, good grammar and spelling are essential here.

CASE STUDY

This will be a fairly in-depth analysis of a complex topic. You will be presented with information in a variety of forms (for instance tables, graphs, newspaper cuttings, correspondence and official reports). You will usually be asked to write a report that summarises the main facts of the case and what the problem is, indicates some possible solutions and outlines your preferred approach – with reasons.

Presentations

Oral presentations are a common assessment tool, especially for jobs where you will be expected to give formal presentations as part of the role. Whatever the subject of your presentation there are some basic principles to bear in mind:

- Keep to the brief
- Practise beforehand
- Structure your talk carefully
- Ensure that you have a clear, effective conclusion
- Consider your audience (likely to consist of your assessors and possibly other candidates too) and pitch your talk according to their level of knowledge and experience in your topic
- If you are allowed visual aids, make good use of them, but don't overuse. For instance, if you are using slides, the slides should just contain highlights or signposts for your talk, not all the detail
- Ensure you don't block the audience's view of visual aids and don't use the screen as your notes – this will result in your talking to the screen, rather than to the group
- It might be useful to produce handouts to give to your audience
- Prompt cards can be useful as an aide-memoire, but do not read your presentation out word for word or learn it off by heart and recite it – both these approaches will sound stilted and unspontaneous
- Speak clearly and project your voice appropriately for the size of the audience and the room. Make sure you don't rush your delivery or speak in a monotone
- Body language is important; maintain a relaxed but confident posture. Resist the temptation to fiddle with hair, pens, etc., as this is likely to distract the audience
- Smile and make eye contact with your audience. Ensure that you include all the audience with your eye contact, though – don't just pick one friendly-looking individual and deliver your presentation to them!
- Anecdotes and examples often give life to a presentation, but be cautious about telling jokes, since the audience may not share your sense of humour!

Group exercises

Whatever form a group exercise takes, there are some basic principles to bear in mind:

- Participate actively in the group, but don't dominate
- Listen and facilitate, encouraging quieter team members to contribute and building on others' ideas
- Bring structure to the exercise and ensure the group doesn't digress. You will probably have a set amount of time for your exercise, so timekeeping is important
- Express yourself clearly and succinctly – avoid waffling or making a comment just for the sake of speaking
- Assessors will appreciate creative thinking – so try to think beyond the obvious, suggesting different angles or approaches to the problem or question in hand
- Present coherent arguments that aim to persuade others of your point of view, but don't be stubborn – be prepared to negotiate.

DISCUSSIONS

Discussions are the most simple and common form of group exercise. You will normally be in a group of five to eight candidates. Someone within the group may be designated as the chair, or it may be a leaderless discussion. You will be asked to discuss one or more topics; these could be issues relevant to the employer or they could be related to current affairs. As a group you may have to choose a topic from a list to discuss. You will be observed by one or more assessors. Before the interview, ensure that you are well informed about current affairs – read broadsheet newspapers, watch and listen to television and radio news.

CASE STUDY

As a group you will be given a business problem. This could be a real-life situation facing the company. Each member of the team may be given a role (e.g. finance, sales or HR manager) and may receive individual briefings on their particular concerns. As a team you must provide a solution, which you may have to then explain in a presentation. (See Written Exercises section for general advice on handling case studies.)

PRACTICAL TASKS

You may be asked as a group to carry out a practical activity (such as constructing a bridge with limited materials). Sometimes different members will be designated varying specialised roles within the team. Although the situation may feel quite different here, the assessors will still be looking for the same kind of characteristics as for other group exercises – so communication and cooperation within your group will be more important than whether you successfully complete the task.

Kurdeep

Having just finished her A-levels, Kurdeep was applying for administrative jobs within law firms.

'I wanted a break before going to university to study law, and I thought it would be a good idea to see what it was like working in the legal environment. I was excited when I had an interview with a couple of firms and, although I thought they went well, I wasn't offered the job. This continued for a while: I kept getting interviews but no jobs. Finally, I was so fed up that I plucked up the courage to telephone a couple of the firms that had interviewed me to try and get some feedback. They both said the same thing: although you met the criteria on paper, you didn't convince us that you really wanted the job.'

Kurdeep had fallen into the trap of assuming that she didn't have to be really enthusiastic about the job because it wasn't her career job, but just a short-term administrative position. The important thing to remember is that often employers are looking for future potential for other jobs, as well as your filling the immediate vacancy now.

case study

8

When the going gets tough: what to do when your job-hunting doesn't bear fruit

This chapter will:

- **show you how to review your job-hunting strategy**
- **give you techniques and sources of information to improve your performance.**

If you are applying for jobs but not getting interviews or job offers, it can be a bit frustrating and dispiriting. What can often happen in a situation like this is you can easily lose all perspective about your abilities, your strategy and your chances of securing the job you want. The important thing is that you take time to reflect on what's actually going on and work out why things aren't going as well as you would like. This chapter will guide you through that process.

Common reasons for failure

Some fundamental questions to ask yourself, so as to work out what's going wrong, include the following:

- Do I really want this job?
- Have I generated enough options?
- Do I have sufficient experience?
- Have I been following up on all leads?
- Have my applications been good enough?
- Is my interview technique good enough?
- Is the job market fairly buoyant in the area I'm interested in?

If you've answered no to any of these questions, it's probably worth revisiting the appropriate chapters of this book which deal with that particular area in detail. But for now, let's go over some of the main reasons for job-hunting failure and what you can do about them.

Not meeting the employer's specifications

It's important for job hunters to err on the side of being optimistic in terms of what they apply for. However, some people fall into the trap of applying for things that they simply haven't got the qualifications for. Some areas of work, for instance, require very good A-levels in specific subjects; others require a degree in a particular subject. Some may even require a specific skill such as knowledge of an obscure foreign language!

Take a moment to review your applications, just to make sure that you have at least two-thirds of the skills or qualities needed for the job. Some employers will send you a 'person specification' related to a job for which you've applied. Often this document will have two columns: one listing essential skills/knowledge that applicants need to do the job; and one listing desirable qualities that applicants should ideally have to do the job. If you are applying for many jobs that stipulate 'essential' skills you don't have, maybe your time is better spent applying for other things.

Another way that you could be damaging your chances without realising it is by not applying for jobs in the right format. We have spent a considerable time going through the process of 'creative' job hunting, but for some positions and sectors you simply have to apply in a certain format. This is often the case with government or civil service jobs, where there is a highly structured application process and applying speculatively with a CV could get you disqualified immediately!

Poor presentation

Poor presentation can come in various forms, ranging from not being professional when you meet employers, to shabby interview technique, to messy formatting on your CVs and covering letters. Again, if you feel that you're guilty of this, take a while to review the chapters on interview technique and making applications.

Some basic guidelines to improve your presentational impact include:

- Always dress smartly when you are meeting an employer (even if it's a recruitment consultant).
- Be enthusiastic and positive and make good eye contact (without overdoing it) during an interview.
- Make sure you appear fresh and well groomed.

When making written applications, try to ensure that you avoid:

- spelling errors
- getting dates wrong
- untidy handwriting
- poor printing/photocopying
- not following the employer's instructions
- using the wrong-coloured ink
- not spending enough time preparing your application.

Falling into the trap of the 'scattergun' approach

Certainly it's important to have a number of job-hunting options to pursue, but sometimes it can be very easy to start applying randomly to many different employers using the same CV and covering letter. This rarely produces results. It's much better to apply to a handful of employers using carefully targeted applications, rather than 30 at random. Ask yourself whether you are trying to do too much. If this is the case, you may need to adjust your job-hunting schedule.

Applications limited to one geographical area

Personal circumstances will sometimes dictate where you live and work. This could restrict your applications and you may have to balance this by being more flexible in your choice of work. Make sure that you fully research your local employment scene and be as proactive as possible in your job search. If you are restricted to a smallish geographical area, you must definitely make speculative approaches rather than just waiting for advertisements. Increasingly, some jobs can be done fully or partially from home. Re-examine the inhibiting factors. Could you arrange things differently or revise travel arrangements?

Strategies for keeping yourself going and improving your chances

Review and renew your skills

You may have identified that one of the reasons you're not having much success is that you lack skills, experience or a qualification in a certain area. If this is the case, you have two choices: first, apply for different things; or second, gain some of the skills needed for the job you want. If you want to develop new skills, the following section shows you how to go about it.

DOING VOLUNTARY WORK
Many people are put off from doing this because obviously it is unpaid, and some are worried that from an employer's point of view it doesn't look good on the CV. Yet nothing could be further from the truth. Employers are less

worried about whether or not you were paid, and more interested in the skills you've developed. Doing voluntary work is a great way to develop some skills that you currently don't possess. As Rebecca Milton, volunteer coordinator at the London School of Economics, comments, 'Volunteering is not only a way of helping others, but a great way of helping yourself, as you will develop skills that will be extremely valuable for your future career.'

To find out more about volunteering opportunities, look in the Yellow Pages or contact your local volunteer bureau. The following organisations may also help:

- National Centre for Volunteering, www.volunteering.org.uk
- Community Service Volunteers, www.csv.org.uk.

TAKING A SHORT COURSE

There are numerous possible courses you could do while you are job hunting, but think carefully about what would be the most valuable thing for you to do. It may be something to develop your IT skills, learning to touch-type, learning the basics of a foreign language, or improving your numeracy. Whatever appeals, and whatever is useful, are worth a try.

Local colleges and adult education centres often offer some courses free of charge (or at least heavily subsidised) for those people who are not yet in employment. Similarly, your local job centre may have some schemes or courses you can enrol in for a very small amount of money, if not free of charge. Another useful source of subsidised courses and training is the government's Learn Direct organisation. You can visit their website at www.learndirect.co.uk or telephone them on 0800 101 901.

CASUAL OR TEMPORARY EMPLOYMENT

Although we've focused on this in an earlier part of the book, it's worth re-emphasising here how important this avenue can be, not only as a possible way into the job you ultimately want, but also as a way of developing your skills and just gaining general work experience. Employment agencies handle many temporary positions in a variety of sectors and organisations, so they can sometimes offer a flexible part-time job that fits in with your job-hunting schedule. One word of caution though: don't take on so much temporary, part-time work that you don't have sufficient time to go after the job you really want!

Keeping your morale up

It's easy to become downhearted if you don't get the job you want, when you want it. The important thing is to keep going and do things to keep your spirits up. The above suggestions will help in this regard, and having a structure to your day is really important. Taking regular exercise is also a good way of remaining positive and energised.

To keep you in high spirits during your job search, you need to develop a support network around you. As well as family and friends, there are several organisations that offer support, such as the following:

CONNEXIONS SERVICES
These organisations offer support and advice (including careers advice) for 13- to 19-year-olds. There should be a branch in your local area. Visit www.connexions.gov.uk for more information.

HIGHER EDUCATION CAREERS SERVICES
If you've been in higher education, you may be able to get access to the institution's careers service, which can often give you invaluable advice and support.

YOUR LOCAL JOB CENTRE
As well as advertising vacancies, there are often lots of support programmes for jobseekers on offer.

Job-huntingtip
Don't always assume that you're doing something wrong if you don't get job offers. It could be bad luck or a very tough job market. Every now and again, do all the checks outlined above and keep going!

Michelle

case study

Following her A-levels, Michelle decided to join the job market. After discussions with her parents, she decided to apply to some high-street banks, because she thought it would be a good idea to get into finance. She looked at a few of their websites and found out what opportunities there were for recent school leavers. Then she made some applications.

'I never realised how long it takes to complete a job application form properly, even though most of them seem to be online.'

The more she found out about it, and the more interviews she had, the less enthusiastic she became about this line of work. 'Once I sat down to think about why I wasn't getting anywhere, I realised that I didn't really want to do this kind of work anyway. It was mainly my parents who pointed me in that direction, but I hadn't thought about it for myself.'

Her lack of enthusiasm during interviews was probably coming across and affecting her performance. After this initial job-hunting period, Michelle spent a long time thinking about her interests and skills and what she really was interested in doing. She eventually decided to apply for jobs in fashion retail, where she now works.

9

Making the change from job hunter to employee

Most books and resources on job hunting examine the process of job hunting only up until you've actually been offered the job or jobs you want. What else is there to do, right? Wrong. There are several issues that need to be considered carefully in order to make the transition into work as smooth and effective as possible. The four main areas that we focus on here are:

- accepting and declining job offers
- making a good first impression at work
- knowing your rights at work
- making the most of your job and boosting your prospects.

Accepting and declining job offers

The process of being offered a job usually happens in the following way:

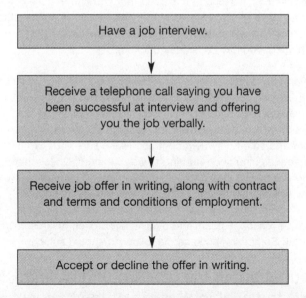

In most cases this process is pretty straightforward, with the majority of applicants delighted to accept the job they've been offered. However, there are a few things worth pointing out. When you are phoned with a job offer, the employer usually asks whether you would like to accept the position. Remember at this point you are in a very strong position to negotiate or ask any questions that weren't necessarily appropriate during an interview. For example, if they haven't been totally clear about the salary you're going to receive, now is the time to ask. Something along the lines of the following might work quite well:

I am very excited by the opportunity and just wondered if you could clarify a couple of things before I formally accept the job.

If the salary is lower than you'd expected it to be, you have two choices: accept the job anyway, or say you'd expected the salary would be slightly higher. If you do want to negotiate a higher salary, this is the best time to try it. You know that they want you; the question is, how much are they prepared to pay? Make sure you have clear reasons why you want a higher salary, though (such as 'most other jobs of a similar nature seem to have a starting salary in the region of X', or you have got experience or skills which are especially relevant or valuable). It's also at this point that you can negotiate your starting date: you may have reasons for wanting to start work on a date other than the one suggested. This will usually be negotiable, especially if you have specific reasons why (e.g. you have a holiday booked).

Making a verbal acceptance of a job in reality is not binding; what's more important is signing and returning the contract which you receive in writing. When you've accepted a job verbally, you are then usually sent some documentation which includes your job description, terms and conditions of employment and an employment contract. Make sure you read everything carefully before signing and returning any documents. Check that there is no disparity between what was offered in the job advertisement and what's being offered now (unless you're being offered more money, of course!).

If, for whatever reason, you have to decline a job offer, make sure you are very polite about it. Something such as the following should suffice:

I've thought about the position and have decided it's not really the right job for me at the moment. I hope this doesn't inconvenience you too much, and thank you for showing an interest in me.

Some lucky applicants get several job offers. In many cases it's obvious which job excites you the most. Sometimes you may be confused and unable to make a decision. If that is the case, go back to the section earlier in the book which discussed values, skills and interests, so that you can be clearer about which job might be best suited to you. Sometimes the timing of job offers and interviews can also cause a problem. The following case study shows this very well:

Rishi

Rishi, a final-year university student, was interested in applying for jobs in the financial field. After spending a lot of time researching companies, making applications and going for some interviews, he received a job offer from a well-known bank.

'I was really pleased to get the offer but also unsure what to do, because I was given two weeks to either accept or decline the offer and I was still going for other job interviews, for jobs I wanted even more than the one I'd been offered. I wasn't sure what to do: if I accepted the job in writing now, could I then write and withdraw at a later date if I got one of the other jobs I wanted even more? I visited my careers service to get advice and another perspective.'

case study

Rishi's case is a tricky one, because it's really impossible to say whether he would get any more job offers. However, a consideration of the following issues would have helped:

- *a careful consideration of whether he really wanted the job he'd been offered* If his only reason for accepting this job was that he feared he wouldn't get another one, that's not necessarily the best way of getting a satisfying job.
- *understanding the notice period for terminating a contract of employment* In any contract of employment, either side has the option of giving notice to terminate it. For staff that have been in post for six months or more, the notice period is up to three months. For newer staff, it can be as little as two weeks.

Now, in Rishi's case, he wasn't actually starting the job until a few months later, after graduation, and even if he had accepted, he could have terminated the contract in writing so long as he had given the exact notice period, even though this would be before the actual start date of the job. So in theory, Rishi could have accepted the first job as a safety net and gone for the other interviews and seen what came of them. This is not good practice, however, and you shouldn't make a habit of doing it to employers; but sometimes a situation dictates that you look after your own interests in ways that might seem duplicitous but which are in fact unavoidable.

Making a good first impression at work

Let's look at the basics of making a good first impression at work and then move on to more subtle matters of settling in and forming good relationships with colleagues:

- Be punctual (but don't leave the office immediately the clock strikes 5!).
- Be enthusiastic.
- Be nice to everyone (but don't be over-familiar too soon).
- Be thorough in your work.

Forming good working relationships with colleagues is very important, but some people find this easier than others, particularly in relation to carrying out 'small talk'. What is small talk? It's about making social chit-chat to break the ice with someone. If you're one of the people who get a bit tongue-tied when it comes to chit-chat, try and make a mental note of the different things you can ask about when you meet someone:

- recreation (what do you do in your spare time?)
- education (where did you go to school?)
- location (where do you live? how long have you been there?)
- family (do you have a family? what does your partner do?)

Usually, these areas will lead on to other areas of conversation. To encourage the conversation to flow, try to ask 'open' questions, but avoid making it sound like an interrogation or a job interview! Questions such as the following should be ok:

- How did you get involved in X?
- What made you decide to do an evening class in Y?
- Where did you work before you came here?

If you are someone who really, really struggles with small talk, you can try another technique, called the A to Z technique. Go through the alphabet in your mind and think of any word beginning with each letter and see if it triggers a thought about which you can have a conversation. For example, you might think of the letter 'A' and think of apples, which might trigger you to think about cider. This could make you think of wine, which in turn triggers a thought about a programme about wine making you saw recently. This technique is a bit random, but it can work really well.

Knowing your rights at work

With any luck, most places you work throughout your career will be pleasant environments and you will be supported and treated fairly. Sometimes, though, employers can try and take liberties at their employees' expense, so it is worth knowing your rights in the workplace. The following list gives you an idea of some of the main areas that you should know about:

Some important employee rights

Common questions	Answers
What is the national minimum wage?	From October 2004, the rates are as follows: 16- and 17-year-olds: £3.00 per hour 18- to 21-year-olds: £4.10 per hour Over 22: £4.85 per hour
What if I'm pregnant? How does that affect my rights at work?	Pregnant women and mothers have various rights to paid and unpaid maternity leave, as well as time off to attend relevant medical appointments. They can also expect to return from maternity leave to work of an equivalent level to that which they did before leaving. They have the right to be treated equally to other employees in other respects, otherwise the employer could be practising sexual discrimination.

If I work part-time, do I have the same rights as full-time employees?	Yes. Part-time workers have the same entitlements to annual leave, pensions, training and other benefits enjoyed by full-time employees at the organisation doing similar work (suitably scaled down according to hours worked).
If I get made redundant, how much severance pay can I get?	Only employees with at least two years' continuous service are legally entitled to redundancy payments. You should be given notice as in your terms and conditions (usually from one to three months), and paid in lieu of this if you do not work it, but anything beyond this is not required by law.
Do recruitment agencies come under the scope of sexual, racial and disability discrimination law?	Yes. At every stage of the employment process, from recruitment and selection to actually doing the job, all are entitled to equal and fair consideration regardless of gender, sexual orientation, race or disability. These requirements cover recruitment consultants as well as employers.
How many hours can an employer make me work in a week?	The Working Time Directive limits a normal working week to no more than 48 hours. This is a maximum, from which you as an employee can opt out. So, by opting out, you are affecting your maximum working hours, not setting a minimum.

For a fuller list of resources about knowing your rights at work, visit the following websites:

■ **Department of Trade & Industry Employment Relations site**
www.dti.gov.uk/er
Lots of useful information on all of the areas covered here, including downloadable resources for employers and employees.

- **TIGER**
  www.tiger.gov.uk
  Another government site offering 'a user-friendly guide through different aspects of employment law'.
- **Inland Revenue**
  www.inlandrevenue.gov.uk/menus/p_taxpayers.htm
  Individual taxpayers' site, including advice on paying tax if you are self-employed.
- **Commission for Racial Equality**
  www.cre.gov.uk
- **Equal Opportunities Commission**
  www.eoc.org.uk
  The experts on equality between men and women at work.
- **Disability Rights Commission**
  www.drc.org.uk
- **Croner Human Resources Centre**
  www.humanresources-centre.net
  Free registration gives access to a wealth of materials on employment-law issues.
- **BBC guide to employment rights**
  www.bbc.co.uk/watchdog/guides_to/employmentlaw/

Making the most of your job and career and boosting your prospects

The first job that most people get is not the one that they will stay in for their whole life. In fact, many people take any sort of job just so that they can get started and get some experience on their CV. Even if your first job isn't your dream job, there are definitely steps you can take to enjoy your work even more, impress others and improve your prospects. Consider the following:

- Once you have got the hang of the basics of your job, look for areas where you can take on extra responsibility, preferably in areas that you would enjoy. See where you can 'grow' your current job.
- Don't fall into the trap of not volunteering to do extra just because you're not paid for it. Most employers will want to see evidence that you can do more before they offer you a better position. Equally, don't become the office dogsbody, so that everybody dumps stuff on you.

- As you did at the beginning of the job-hunting process, analyse where you have some gaps in your skills and knowledge and try to get some experience in those areas.
- If you have a really good idea for work, put forward a proposal to your manager and see what they think of it.
- Use your initiative and be proactive.

These points, if implemented, should show you at your best at work and ensure that you have a successful career. Employers always respond well to people who are enthusiastic and who are willing to 'put themselves into' their job. This kind of attitude will stand you in good stead and will create opportunities for you: opportunities that could take your career in directions you may not have even thought of or considered before.

I hope you will be ready to take them when they appear.

Further reading and weblinks

Books

Winning CVs for First-time Job Hunters, 2nd edition, Kathleen Houston, Trotman Publishing

Winning Interviews for First-time Job Hunters, Kathleen Houston, Trotman Publishing

Job Hunting for Dummies, Max Messmer, IDG Books

Careers 2005, Trotman Publishing

Perfect Job Search Strategies, Tom Jackson, Piatkus Books

The A to Z of Careers and Jobs, Kogan Page Books

The Penguin Careers Guide, Anna Alston & Anne Daniel, Penguin Books

Websites

www.trotman.co.uk is the site for Trotman Publishing. Has lots of useful careers information for people of all ages.

www.careers.lon.ac.uk is the home page of the University of London Careers Service. Check out in particular the Virtual Careers Library, which has many links to information about different occupations and careers.

www.prospects.ac.uk is another site mainly aimed at students and graduates, but there are lots of useful elements to it.

www.learndirect.co.uk is a government site giving details of subsidised courses and training.

www.volunteering.org.uk is the website for the National Centre for Volunteering.

www.csv.org.uk is the homepage of Community Service Volunteers.

SELECTED JOB RECRUITMENT SITES
www.workthing.com
www.monster.co.uk
www.alljobsuk.com
www.fish4jobs.co.uk
www.totaljobs.com
www.hotrecruit.co.uk

SELECTED SITES ABOUT EMPLOYMENT-RELATED ISSUES

www.tiger.gov.uk is a government site offering a user-friendly guide to different aspects of employment law.

www.cre.gov.uk is the home page for the Commission for Racial Equality.

www.eoc.org.uk is a site about equality between men and women at work.

www.drc.org.uk is the website of the Disability Rights Commission.